About the Author

Greg Bogart, Ph.D., MFT, is a psychotherapist and astrological counselor in the San Francisco Bay Area. He teaches in the Counseling Psychology and East-West Psychology programs at the California Institute of Intergral Studies (CIIS). He is also a Lecturer in psychology at Sonoma State University. His books include *Planets in Therapy, Astrology and Spiritual Awakening*, and *Dreamwork and Self-Healing:Unfolding the Symbols of the Unconscious.*

Astrology and Meditation

The Fearless Contemplation of Change

Greg Bogart

Published in England in 2002 by
The Wessex Astrologer Ltd
4A Woodside Road
Bournemouth
BH5 2AZ
England

www.wessexastrologer.com

ISBN 1902405129

Printed and bound in the UK by Biddles Ltd.,
Guildford and King's Lynn

2nd printing 2012

A catalogue record for this book is available
at the British Library

Acknowledgments

I would like to express my gratitude to my wonderful friends and colleagues: Sid Aaronson, Rick Amaro, Stephanie Austin, Ken Bowser, Marka Carson, Linda Cogozzo, Cathy Coleman, Richard Cook, Patty Davidson, Sangye Drolma, Jennifer Freed, Karen Fry, Rob Gellman, Demetra George, Carolyn and Roy Gillett, Ken Gilman, Ray Grasse, Dennis Harness, Peta High, Ken Irving, David Kesten, Michael Lutin, Neil Marbell, Colleen Mauro, Mark McNutt, Ray Merriman, Barbara Morgan, Bob Mulligan, Claude Palmer, Glenn Perry, Kim Phelps, Steve Pincus, Laura Shekerjian, Barbara Somerfield, Georgia Stathis, Jonathan Tenney, and Stuart Walker. I would also like to think the publisher and staff of *The Mountain Astrologer*: Tem Tarriktar, Kate Sholly, Mary Plumb, and Nan Geary.

For the past two decades, Shelley Jordan and I have been studying astrology together and discussing our work. Shelley spent countless hours with me on the telephone reviewing the manuscript of this book, poring over charts, challenging me, and offering her insights.

I am grateful to Margaret Cahill, who has made it possible for this book to come to fruition. I would also like to acknowledge my astrology teachers, Patricia Stauffer, Andrés Takra, Dane Rudhyar, and Chakrapani Ullal, for all their wisdom and generosity. And loving thanks to Diana Syverud, whose humor, intuition, and joyous spirit light my way.

Portions of this book previously appeared in *The Mountain Astrologer*, and *The International Astrologer*.

The names of all clients discussed in this book have been changed and minor details altered to protect anonymity. I would like to thank each of these individuals for their commitment to the process of self-transformation.

This book was completed December 31, 2001, Full Moon Eclipse in Cancer, conjunct Jupiter. May it be of benefit to sentient beings everywhere.

Also by Greg Bogart

Astrology and Spiritual Awakening

*Therapeutic Astrology: Using the Birth Chart in Psychotherapy
and Spiritual Counselling*

Finding Your Life's Calling: Spiritual Dimensions of Vocational Choice

*The Nine Stages of Spiritual Apprenticeship: Understanding
the Student-Teacher Relationship*

Dreamwork and Self-Healing:Unfolding the Symbols of the Unconscious

To the consciousness that has realized the existence of cycles and is able to shift gears from the profane to the sacred, the whole of living becomes imbued with the magic of eternity. Every event is accepted as a necessary phase of the ritual process of existence radiating at every moment the significance and inner peace that wells out from the security of knowing oneself to be an essential and operative part of a vast cyclic whole. This is the symbolic life. It is also the life of wisdom, for to be wise is to know with unimpeachable knowing that the whole is fulfilling itself at every moment through and within every act of life, once this life, illumined by nonpossessive love, is rooted in the certainty that order, beauty, rhythmic interplay and the harmony of ever balanced opposites are here and now, indestructibly.

Dane Rudhyar [1]

Contents

1

Astrology, Meditation, and the Fearless Contemplation of Change

I honor the light within you. In this book we are going to explore how the sacred art of astrology can help us find our way and become awakened human beings. We are indeed fortunate to have the direct guidance from the universe that we get from astrology, which leads us through a lifelong training for enlightenment. Through the wisdom of astrology, may we reach our goal of fully unfolding our evolutionary potential!

I have always viewed astrology not so much as a means of prediction but as a tool for the evolution of consciousness. It is a contemplative discipline: We meditate on our charts, and watch ourselves unfolding like deities taking form before our inner eye; and we actively participate in the embodiment of spiritual archetypes. Each transit is a step toward fuller incarnation of the deity, the Self, the essence that we are. Moreover, astrology brings the sacred right into the heart of the profane, into our everyday lives. The divine intelligence is felt in every moment and every movement of evolution.

The mature practice of astrology is defined not so much by a set of techniques as it is by an attitude or stance. Ultimately the most power-ful astrological technique is not progressions or solar returns, midpoints, harmonics or *dasa* periods. The most powerful astrological "technique" is a quiet mind, a stance of contemplation. No matter which techniques we use, when our minds are agitated our studies of astrology result in fear of the future, of malefic planets, and of challenging aspects or transits. When our minds are clear and quiet, we begin to discern the meaning of even the most tumultuous events in our lives so that we remain centered, calm, and hopeful. Thus, I consider a personal meditation practice one of the keys to a positive, growth-oriented approach to the celestial art.

All too often I speak with people who have been terrorized by dismal and often irresponsible astrological predictions. For example, Gwen had been told by an astrologer that she was likely to die or suffer other catastrophes because transiting Pluto was conjunct her Sun. While transiting Pluto may manifest through crisis events, often this crisis is one that leads to profound growth and transformation. During this transit, the crisis Gwen encountered was a hostile corporate takeover of the company where she worked. She skillfully positioned herself so that she ended up in a better position within the reorganized company. During the transit she became stronger, tougher, wiser about the ways of power in the world. Not only was the prediction of death completely wrong but it also completely failed to see the deeper dimensions and growth potential of the Pluto transit.

The purpose of this book is to explore how we can go beyond the traditional black and white, malefic-benefic way of thinking about astrological influences. One famous astrologer told me the period when transiting Saturn was conjunct my Venus would be "bad for relationships." This simplistic statement failed to grasp or convey the complexity of that period and the growth that I experienced in my capacity to relate in a mature and committed way. I was determined to look at my fears and to master them (Saturn). The prediction was, in fact, wrong. I got involved in a stable and loving relationship at that time. As students of astrology, we try to understand the purpose of each event in furthering our growth. The key is a meditative attitude. Another key is the ability to look at any chart symbol in a number of ways, chewing it over and digesting it thoroughly, looking at it from many angles and reflecting on its *many* possible meanings. I'll discuss this later in the chapter on Symbol Amplification.

Astrology is the art of contemplating the ever-changing moments of time. As we gain proficiency in prediction, we also begin to discern what the predicted events might *mean*. We begin to approach study of the birth chart as a form of active meditation where we contemplate whatever we see coming up astrologically, or happening right now, with an attitude of quiet expectation and receptivity to whatever wants to unfold. The deepest meaning of planetary symbols is discovered through personal revelation, through the astrological meditation practice where we sit with a quiet mind and contemplate natal chart symbols, or a current or upcoming transit or progression.

The first thing I am going to ask you to do, right now, is to take a few breaths. If you want to deepen your state of consciousness and your study of astrology, begin by opening up the breath. I am amazed that no one else has stated this before—that the breath is an important tool in the practice of astrology. As your breath deepens, let the mind's turbulence quiet down until your awareness plunges deeply within, deep into the ocean of Consciousness. As you contemplate your natal planets and current transits, breathe, and ask, "What is the purpose of this? What is the highest potential manifestation of this celestial symbol? What is the secret intention of this process? What is the most positive outcome I can imagine?" Keep breathing, and be open to receiving new insight from within. As Dane Rudhyar once wrote,

> The astrological chart is ... not something merely to be studied with a coldly analytical intellect. It is something to be *felt* ... Face the chart as an artist faces a painting, in positive and keenly aware openness to it, with the eager determination to *evoke* the significance of it—and to help the client to reach a fuller state of conscious integration. Face the chart with full acceptance of personal responsibility—and indeed in an attitude of "prayer," asking for inner guidance and the bestowal of wise understanding.[2]

This meditative, contemplative astrology is different from the astrology of dread and fear, where we passively suffer the effects of the planets.[3] We begin to search for the positive evolutionary intent and purpose of every event, even the most painful ones. Does transiting Saturn conjunct or square Venus mean a terrible period of failure in relationship? Or is it an indicator that this is a time in which our capacity for maturity in relationships will be developed and tested? *We have the power to choose the meaning of our planetary placements and transits.* While traditional astrology viewed Saturn as a malefic planet, we now recognize that Saturn is the planet that can lead us toward stability, maturity, and responsibility. As our understanding of the celestial art grows, we enthusiastically embrace each challenging transit and try to find positive meaning in it. We use astrology to help ourselves and others meet change with courage.

The main obstacle to astrological enlightenment is fear. We fear the transits or progressions that we are passing through instead of embracing them as initiatory lessons. A man named Frank, a lawyer, had transiting

Pluto conjunct natal Mars in Sagittarius, in the 10th house (Chart #1). He consulted with an astrologer who told him it was going to be a difficult period in which he might come under attack. The astrologer told him, "Your life will be hell until December." No further explanation was offered. Indeed things did get intense for Frank. First he got into a fight with a man at the health club during a basketball game; he was bruised physically and emotionally. He started working out obsessively with weights until he got really enormous. Then someone at his law firm beat him out for inside position on a big case. Frank was livid, seething with jealousy, and preoccupied with fantasies of revenge. He said, "That's twice now I've been burned by men who have wielded power over me and injured my body, my career, my pride." The astrologer's prediction of attack seemed as if it was manifesting. Then he had a Plutonian eruption: He got furious and flew off the handle at a meeting, damaging his reputation in his firm. At home, he had a tantrum and broke a glass window. He had an outbreak of a rash all over his body. He had migraine headaches. He was miserable. All he wanted to know was when this awful period would be over. I said, "Instead of just waiting it out, why don't you try to understand the purpose of this transit and the lessons it may hold for you?"

I asked Frank to meditate deeply in silence and then to contemplate the potential outcome of this transit, what kind of metamorphosis was intended, and possible, for him at this time. I informed him that, with Pluto conjunct natal Mars, he was in the midst of a deep transformation of his masculine identity, his competitiveness and anger, and his attitude toward power; and he had an opportunity to learn a more positive expression of his energy and motivation through his career (Mars in 10th house). I said, "A great deal of power and energy can become available to you during this transit (Pluto conjunct Mars), but you need to decide whether to direct it toward your adversaries or toward making a positive contribution to the world." I asked him if he could invoke in his mind's eye any images of male identity that were inspiring to him. He named several sports heroes, rock stars, and ambitious politicians. He also spoke of his admiration for some of the more ruthless senior lawyers in his firm. But he realized that none of these was truly an image of his own most evolved ideal. Then he glimpsed an image of a man traveling extensively and committed to social justice. This was surprising and intriguing to him.

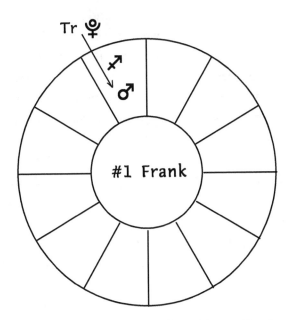

Over the course of several weeks after this meditation, Frank began to envision himself being transformed into a highly ethical lawyer working to alleviate suffering. Two months later, he quit his job and went to work for an international human rights organization. He was thorough, completely committed, and zealously energetic about this work. His anger, his energy, and his competitiveness got channeled into this meaningful project. He began to do work for the service of humanity, instead of striving for power and recognition. Frank's physical symptoms mysteriously disappeared, just as they do when you take the correct homeopathic remedy. A change of attitude toward a difficult transit can be very potent. This is an example of how, through a meditative approach to astrological symbolism, we project an image forward into the future and gradually mold ourselves into its embodiment.

In *Astrology and Spiritual Awakening* I described the *kriya shakti*, the power to imagine and visualize and thereby shape our future unfolding. We envision the next stage of our personal metamorphosis and allow this ideal to become what Rudhyar called "an irrefutable reality for the consciousness and a steady, indestructible commitment."[4]

To access this power in astrology we approach the chart in a contemplative manner, allowing celestial archetypes and symbols to sharpen the clarity of our intuition. We sit quietly with a silent mind and contemplate a transit that corresponds to some difficulty we are facing, and ask, "What is the highest potential outcome or manifestation of this planetary symbol? What is the secret intention of this process?" When asked this question, a man with transiting Neptune entering his 2nd house, who was suddenly making less money, told me, "To be simpler and less materialistic." A man with progressed Mars square Saturn responded: "To be less sexually obsessed and fixated." A woman with transiting Pluto conjunct Saturn and who was going through difficult times, said, "I've never really faced adversity before. I know this is making me stronger." In the practice of astrological meditation we reflect on how, given the planetary influences of this moment, we can use our present experience as a step forward in our evolution. In our hearts we know what is being asked of us, even where we resist the lessons life is offering us.

Astrology is the path of harvesting meaning from events, consuming life experience as food, even difficult experiences. We stop cursing our lives. We are ready for anything. The great astrologer Grant Lewi foresaw his own death from his horoscope and calmly went about the business of saying goodbye to friends and making financial arrangements for his family. He was detached, realistic, and free of self-pity.[5] Astrology teaches us to be at peace no matter where we are. We begin to live with heightened awareness of the meaning and purpose of each event within the cycles of our evolution. We start to understand who we are supposed to become, the tests we must face, and the tasks we must fulfill. And so paradoxically, while we learn to choose and mold, through our visualization, the meaning of our natal chart symbolism, our transits and progressions, we also begin to be more at peace with the way things unfold. We rest in the state of just being, in the stillness of consciousness beyond thought, beyond struggle. Everything is as it is. We accept whatever unfolds with evenmindedness.

A few years ago I had a lot of Mars activity in my chart—solar arc Uranus square natal Mars; transiting Mars retrograde square natal Mars; progressed Moon opposite natal Mars; a lunar return with Mars on the Ascendant and natal Mars on the IC. I was aware that something might happen that would cause a little pain. I just hoped and prayed that it wouldn't lead to serious injury or loss of friends or angry confrontations with others. I assiduously avoided skiing or other dangerous sports activities. I was extra careful while handling power tools and appliances as I didn't want to start any fires or accidentally hack off anything. I drove more cautiously. I was careful, on the lookout for the incident, the accident, knowing that somehow it would probably find me anyway. When a client stiffed me several hundred dollars on some work I had done for her, I kept my composure. I didn't fly off the handle, even though I was hurt and quietly angry about it. I wrote her a letter that was direct and firm, polite and not at all combative or insulting. I thought, "I'm home free. I've successfully neutralized Mars by being such a nice guy." I had met aggression without aggression of my own. But Mars was not finished with me quite yet. The next morning I slipped and fell on the deck outside my home, badly bruising my ribcage. Instantly I knew that this was it. I could not breathe, sit, lie down, or move without intense pain. I witnessed the pain. It continued. I continued to witness it, to live it through without resisting it. I let the knife of Mars pierce me, wound me. I assented to it. In his book *An Astrological Triptych*, Dane Rudhyar wrote:

> Man is man through the challenge of the earth, meeting which, he calls upon himself the release of spirit from the heart of divine plenitude. . . . Man experiences through nature. He rises through nature. Not against, but through. . . . The hand passes through the water. It experiences the water, the fluidity of it, yet it emerges from it, still a hand — the integrity of a hand, *plus* consciousness from the experience. Consciousness is through-ness. It is born of thoroughness of experiencing.[6]

Reflection on planetary symbolism enables us to meet "the challenge of the earth," to move through each life experience with consciousness, fearlessness, and openness to change. In this moment, in each and every Now, perfection is unfolding.

The Mandala Principle in Astro-Meditation

Rudhyar often described the astrological chart as a mandala, a centering diagram and an object of contemplation. Reflecting on the birth chart in a meditative frame of mind evokes the mandala principle, the process by which astrology brings us to our center. As we contemplate the chart we are enlightened by it; some new insight is always revealed to us. Personally I find the ritual practice of drawing out the birth chart by hand especially helpful. To deepen your practice of astrology and meditation, breathe and allow your mind to become quiet, then draw your birth chart by hand. Do this mindfully, as a centering act. Contemplate the chart as you draw it. As you draw the wheel of the houses feel the totality of experience, the mandala of human concerns. As you draw each planet sense your attunement or current level of responsiveness to that planet. Do you feel in balance with that planet's energies? Does it need more attention?

In the gesture of drawing the circle of the chart we invoke wholeness, the totality of the cycle and its phases. We center ourselves, and we stand at the crossroads where all opposites coexist. This is the *bindu*, the point of consciousness. In a simple sweep of the hand we draw the circle of houses and create the mandala of orientation. We feel the cross of self and other (Ascendant and Descendant), root and flower, earth and sky (IC/MC). We feel the tension or union of opposites within ourselves as we draw our interplanetary aspects. We sense where current energies are focused, and where they will be focused in the future. I often reflect on this passage from Carl Jung's *Memories, Dreams, Reflections*:

> When I began drawing the mandalas... I saw that everything, all the paths I had taken, were leading back to a single point—namely to the midpoint. It became increasingly plain to me that the mandala is the center... It is the path to the center, to individuation... There is no linear evolution; there is only a circumambulation of the Self.[7]

Following our transits around the birth chart is circumambulation of the Self, the wholeness that we potentially are. Jung said that mandalas represent the totality of the psyche. Similarly, the astrological birth chart drawn with current transits represents to us the current condition of the psyche. We feel the balance or chaos of internal and external forces at play in our lives. The birth chart is a mandala, representing the wholeness of the psyche, the totality of all we are and can potentially be. But it is up to us, the human intermediaries, to make archetypal potentials and our envisioned goals a tangible reality.

2

Astrological Yoga and Planetary Meditations

Now let us meditate on the spiritual lessons of the signs and planets, and reflect on how we can more impeccably and courageously fulfill the instructions that our birth charts encode and convey. We are going to do basic meat and potatoes astrology—no fancy techniques—but always reflecting on how we can use every experience to become more fully unfolded beings. I focus on the planets in signs and houses, transits, secondary progressions, and solar arc directions because I believe the essence of all we need to know is available from these core symbols. I also discuss planetary pairs and midpoints. While I am quite interested in more advanced astrological methods, I find that the most profound meanings are usually found by deeply contemplating the most elementary planetary symbols.

As we advance in our studies of astrology, we become centered and prepared to meet whatever comes. We awaken through every experience, meeting each moment with courage. We also learn to use our will to shape what unfolds, acting in accordance with our planetary instruction manual. We have to deal with our personal problems and resolve to change them. If transiting Saturn is entering the 2nd house and our finances aren't so great, we don't give up and say I can't possibly improve my situation because of Saturn. We take it as an imperative message to make strong efforts in that direction. That is precisely what we need to work on. We need to take responsibility for our lives, and not use our planets as an excuse for lack of effort. It's totally up to us what we make of the evolutionary opportunities astrology and life present to us.

Astrology teaches us that there are infinitely varied ways to be an awakened human being, and it encourages us to embrace our own path. It reveals the *yoga*, the spiritual practice or life-road that best suits us, and the steps we need to take to come into greater balance.[8]

Through the study of astrology we learn that there are moments of a specific duration that have a particular theme or tone. Certain types of experiences are likely to occur under the influence of the various planets: Mercury—the stimulation of new ideas. Saturn—work and responsibility; Venus—love, aesthetic enjoyment, and sensual pleasure. We develop a sense of how long these experiences may last. We learn not to freeze any moment or experience or emotional state into permanence. Everything is changing. Reflecting on the ever-changing celestial pattern, we start to live as the Witness, the one who sees all with compassion. At the center of the chart is the Self, I Am, the field of consciousness. We are the *purusha*—the tranquil, eternal Being, not the constantly changing flux of events. Events change. We are unchanging Presence. Our awareness shifts and evolves through each experience; everything is given to us as a gift, a lesson. I witness myself going through a variety of experiences, some pleasurable, some boring or tedious, some exciting, some gut-wrenching. But none of these experiences is what I am. I am the consciousness that grows through the totality of all experience. I dispassionately witness what happens, and through each experience my consciousness expands.

Astrology is the study of the orderly unfolding of the universe. The planetary cycles proceed according to their intelligent and relatively predictable course. Our goal is to align ourselves with the larger rhythms of life. We experience disharmony when we are out of tune with these planetary cycles, with the natural rhythm in which things want, and *intend*, to happen. We want Neptunian bliss at the moment when the universe is calling for grounded attention to our feelings or relationships, or to the home or workplace. Our task is to tune ourselves to the vibration of each planet, responding to each, as needed, to master the level of consciousness that each planet represents; and to embody each natal planet, especially as it is activated by transits and progressions. As we do so, we gradually become more whole and integrated human beings—complex, multidimensional, fully actualized on every level.[9]

The Sun

Our first task is to know who we are as individuals, to express an inner cohesion and clear sense of self that is symbolized by the natal Sun. The Sun represents our conscious identity, that way of being in which we are most fully alive, creative, and filled with light. The Sun is what yogis call *ahamkara*, the I-sense. It can manifest as egoic self-preoccupation without any awareness of the deeper spiritual and archetypal ground of our existence. But as it is transformed through response to the outer planets, the Sun identifies how we focus the creative energies of Spirit as an organized center of activity and awareness, through our radiant individuality. The Sun is the power to emanate from our true center, radiating the warmth of love, and the joy of Being, through the personality. Our goal is to project the clear light of our central solar ray. Each of the twelve Sun signs is a *yoga*, a spiritual path, a life road or path to the Source—as discussed in Appendix A.

A central goal of this incarnation is to be most fully and consciously a Taurean, a Libran, an Aquarian type of person. A man with Capricorn Sun dropped out of his corporate career to bum around in Asia after transiting Neptune was conjunct his Sun. But within a few months he grew bored with this and came home to resume pursuit of his career and ambitions. This was his true path. A 46-year-old widow with Sun in Libra (and Moon in the 7th house) was in a quandary when men started asking her on dates. She said, "I'm through with relationships, I don't want to get into another one." Yet relationships kept seeking her. She may need to accept that being in relationship was a prominent, even a necessary condition of her evolution. In contrast, a woman named Ellen with Sun in Pisces (in the 11th house) complained of her loneliness and isolation as a single mother (Chart #2).

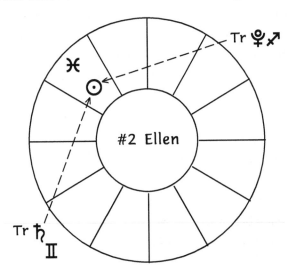

During our consultation she was only interested in knowing about when she would meet someone and fall in love. Unfortunately, I could find no current indicators suggesting this in the immediate future. The great British astrologer William Lilly describes how some of his astrological competitors would lie to their clients and give them positive readings because otherwise the clients would not pay![10] But to be effective astrologers one of the qualities we need is radical honesty; otherwise astrology becomes a sham. I noted that a transiting Saturn-Pluto opposition was heading into a lengthy square to her natal Sun. I told Ellen I felt life was being quite insistent that right now she fulfill her evolutionary purpose as a Pisces by developing her spirituality. I explained that the Pisces moment of evolution is different from the Libra moment of loving union with another. It is about finding the peace and stillness that exists regardless of whether or not we have a particular type of relationship. At first, she didn't like hearing this, but later she said these words resonated with a deep part of her. Relationship indicators seemed more promising a bit in the future; but for this moment she had to decide whether to wallow in self-pity and loneliness, or to find her connection with God and to consciously emanate a serene inner light. We identified many ways she could cultivate contentment in her daily life, and we determined that it was her destiny, and her choice, to become a woman of peaceful clarity. From this place she could attract love in due time. The bottom line is that we need to live our solar archetype consciously.

A 26-year-old woman with Sun in Scorpio at the Midheaven was terrified of her chart, and hated the symbolism of Scorpio. She was from a Muslim family in which women were expected to be subservient and docile. She was neither. She was conflicted about being a strong, assertive woman with intense sexual feelings. It was contrary to her social conditioning. When transiting Uranus squared her Sun she had a dream involving a black cat, a black rabbit, and a black snake, which bit her. To her, the cat represented intuition and acting on her instincts, the rabbit was a positive symbol of sexuality, and the snake represented the expression of her outspokenness, anger, and personal power. When the snake bit her in the dream, at first she panicked, but then she realized that the snake's venom wasn't dangerous to her. In fact, it made her stronger. Working with these dream symbols helped her accept, and live, her Scorpio nature.

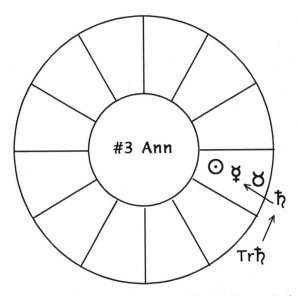

Also, we need to actualize our solar way of being through the natal house or field of life in which the Sun is placed. For example, a client of mine named Ann with the Sun-Mercury in Taurus in her 6th house had been working all her life (Chart #3). Ann had her first baby while Saturn passed through her 5th house and she thought that she wanted to have two or three babies and quit working. But when transiting Saturn went into her 6th house a year later, she decided to go back to work. Ann was racked with guilt and afraid that she was letting down her child by working. She knew about John Bowlby's attachment theory and the problems that may result from lengthy separation of mother and child, but perhaps she was making a bit too much of this, exaggerating the risk.[11] The reality was that the family needed her income and she herself was restless to go back to work. Her 6th house Sun needed this. She was a worker. It was the right way for her to follow. We need to stay in alignment with the purpose and natural way of being indicated by our natal Sun. Ellen, the woman with Pisces Sun in the 11th house (Chart #2), needed to explore spirituality within the context of a group or community. I have the Sun in my 4th house, so I can barely be budged from my home, a fact to which all my friends will attest. Understanding the placement of the Sun is fundamental. Every astrologer should be able to make a clear statement about the meaning of our natal Sun sign and house placement and what this says about who we are.

We should also have an understanding of the natal Sun's aspects, which tell us which planetary principles are likely to be accentuated in our evolution. For example, with Sun-Mars aspects we may exhibit strong will and personal initiative, energy, strength, decisiveness, or combativeness.[12] Sun-Jupiter aspects may highlight travel, education, and intellectual achievement —along with qualities such as carelessness, extravagance, or blind optimism.[13] Sun-Saturn aspects emphasize hard work, overcoming fear, shyness, and self-doubt, so that we can focus, achieve, and bear responsibility (Saturn).[14] Sun aspects to the outer planets (Uranus, Neptune, and Pluto), represent our responsiveness to forces initiating us into expanded consciousness.

As we contemplate the Sun and the formation of the ego we begin to consider what purpose it serves. We realize that the individual ego is not an end in itself, for it must always be meaningfully related to something greater than itself. Astrology teaches us to become functional wholes within a greater whole, a larger field of being—within our family, community, nation, planet. Of course this means being functional within society, at the Saturn level. But also, the Sun, the individual ego identity, is to act as a vessel for the light of the Whole, the galaxy, whose "ambassadors" are the outer planets.[15] Sun aspects to Uranus symbolize rebelliousness, independence from the dominant culture, expression of our uniqueness, and originality. Sun-Neptune aspects signify intuition, imagination, compassion, developing a spiritual and self-transcending intention. Sun-Pluto aspects test us to over-come ego impurities—our sense of superiority, intense need for attention, or for dominance over others, or our self-destructive tendencies—so that we can powerfully express the essence of who we are. Without a self-transcending motive or intention as a guiding principle for our lives, we become lost in self-glorification and attention-seeking, greed and materialism, or the mass fascination with celebrity and scandal—the Plutonian black hole. Astrology shows us a higher path, a path of spiritual and planetary service.

The Moon

To become vessels of the Light of Being we need to be emotionally healthy and self-aware, in touch with our core feelings and understanding the quality of our emotional attachments with others, symbolized by the natal Moon. Our natal Moon placement helps us understand our emotions, innermost

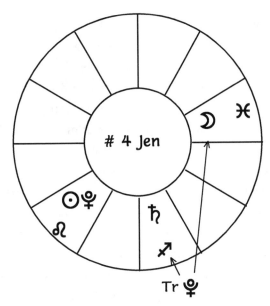

needs, and dominant feeling states. A woman with a natal conjunction of Moon, Saturn, and Neptune in Libra in the 8th house had a manic demeanor, laughing constantly as she described her struggles in life. She began to cry as we explored her underlying feelings of sadness, depression, desolation, and sense of abandonment in relationships. "Yes," she said, "this is the dominant feeling state I return to again and again."

Transits to the Moon are opportunities to revisit and heal old emotional wounds. For example, Pluto transits to the natal Moon often denote emotional upheavals and surfacing of resentments that make it possible for us to heal the past and move freely into the present moment and all of its possibilities. A client named Jen had transiting Pluto squaring her natal Pisces Moon in the 7th house and conjunct natal Saturn in Sagittarius (Chart #4). Focusing on the 7th house placement of her Pisces Moon, I asked Jen about her marriage. She said her husband, Edward, has a drinking problem and has been sober for just three months, and that she has been feeling quite isolated from him. She has also supported him financially for several years. I asked about her relationship with her mother (Moon), curious how this might be relevant to her feelings about Edward. Jen felt emotionally abandoned by her mother, whom she said had always acted like a martyr (Moon in Pisces). But now Jen was playing the martyr in her own marriage, feeling abandoned by Edward, who was preoccupied with his job struggles and never found time to sit down and talk with her. Jen described her mother as very traditional, repressed, rigid, serious, stern (Moon square Saturn). Dad, on the other hand, was boisterous, fun-loving, immature, irresponsible, especially about money. Note her Sun-Pluto conjunction in Leo in her 2nd house, which is the 5th house from the father 10th. Her father was a compulsive gambler,[16] and Jen told me that she herself shopped and spent money too freely and had run up enormous credit card debts (Pluto in 2nd). Was it possible, I wondered, that she shopped compulsively to compensate for her sadness and feelings of emptiness in her marriage? With Saturn in her 4th house (square Moon in 7th), family of origin issues were being reenacted in marriage; Jen felt she was playing the role of her stern, disapproving mother while Edward played her father's role as the irresponsible alcoholic.

With Pluto square natal Moon, lots of emotions were surfacing in their marriage. Jen felt resentment about standing by Edward all those years while he was drinking, all the while feeling like he wasn't present emotionally, as well as not pulling his weight financially. It was time to peel back the layers of denial, avoidance, and depression in her marriage (transiting Pluto square Pisces Moon, square Saturn). Together we practiced the astrological meditation described earlier, asking, "What is the highest outcome of this transit?" I prompted her, saying, "Maybe it means your marriage could become more emotionally supportive and nurturing." I added that perhaps the transit was an opportunity to develop more emotional openness, honesty, and vulnerability, and to clear the resentments and emotional blocks that were in the way. Slowly things began to improve. Jen got Edward to go to couples therapy, and they did some deep work together. Edward found a job, and became more attentive. Jen felt closer to him. This example illustrates how astrology can help transform our lives by enabling us to envision a positive end state or goal of every transit process. Envisioning the end state helps us steer ourselves toward precisely that goal—in this case, the goal of emotional union symbolized by Pisces Moon in the 7th house.

Mercury

Mercury represents the mind, intelligence and learning, the endless curiosity to know. Attuning to Mercury, we develop our minds, our ability to find information and communicate our ideas effectively. A woman with a natal

Mercury-Neptune conjunction in her 3rd house spends much of her free time reading metaphysical books and writing poetry. A man with transiting Saturn conjunct natal Mercury is writing his doctoral dissertation, learning how to organize his ideas and present them in an acceptable academic form. A woman named Liz had transiting Pluto square natal Mercury in Virgo (Chart #5). She described her current state as wired, high strung, nervous, with her mind racing out of control, restless to learn. It so happened that at the same time she had progressed Mars quincunx Pluto and she broke her foot while traveling abroad. She was currently convalescing at home with her leg in a cast, spending all of her time reading dozens of books.

Developing our Mercury functions we become more informed, more articulate, more intelligent. I find it quite helpful to follow the transit cycle of Mercury in its relationship to the Sun throughout the year. We note that when Mercury turns retrograde a particular task, issue, or problem occupies our attention. During the retrograde period we have the opportunity to rethink the problem and to gather new information that may be helpful to us. Note the sign and house in which Mercury retrograde conjoins the Sun (this is called the "inferior conjunction") and then eventually completes its retrograde period and turns direct in motion. The placement of the Sun-Mercury conjunction identifies areas of our lives that occupy our attention fully for this period of time. Rather than viewing Mercury retrograde

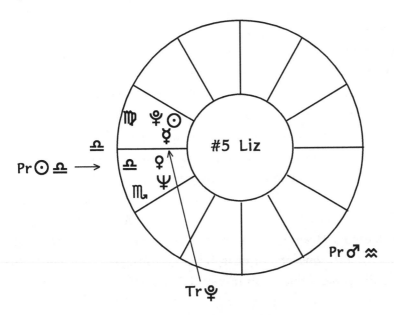

periods as times of impossible muddle-headedness when we should avoid making all important decisions (a view often espoused by those practicing fear-based astrology in its most banal form), I consider these to be periods when we can make tremendous progress with our lives by reconsidering problems we are facing, and actively searching for new solutions and ideas. In *Therapeutic Astrology* I wrote,

> The sign and house placement in which a Sun-Mercury inferior conjunction occurs indicates the area of life requiring the most focused mental attention and effort at this time. For example, during a Sun-Mercury conjunction in the 4th house, we may put more energy into decisions affecting our home, domestic environment, garden, or communication with our family. A Sun-Mercury conjunction in the 9th house may seek expression through intellectual activity focused on a search for truth and meaning through study or travel. With the conjunction in the 10th house, professional demands require focused attention and new insight. One man took driving lessons for the first time at the age of thirty-four during a Sun-Mercury conjunction in his 3rd house. A songwriter experienced a burst of creativity during a Sun-Mercury conjunction in her 5th house. A woman reorganized her personal finances during a conjunction in her 2nd house.[17]

Attunement to Mercury's transit cycle helps us know where and when to focus our attention, so that we can coordinate many projects and areas of life and function at peak efficiency.

Mercury's aspects inform us about various facets of the process of developing a refined intellect. Natal aspects or transits of Jupiter to Mercury support growth of knowledge through reading, studies, and enhance our expression in speech and writing. Most of the writers, scholars, and intellectuals that I know have strong aspects of Mercury and Jupiter. Mercury gains focus, organization, and practicality through contacts with Saturn. Saturn's transits to Mercury are often times demanding clear logic, grounded thinking, and strategic decision-making. Aspects of Uranus to Mercury refer to the evolution of our genius, inventiveness, and original ideas. A man with a Mercury-Uranus conjunction in the 11th house showed flashes of great brilliance in his writing, which was political in focus (11th house). A woman with Mercury-Uranus conjunct in Virgo in the 1st house had highly unusual, idiosyncratic speech patterns, often inventing her own words. She was a healthcare professional with unusual diagnostic acumen (Virgo).

Mercury-Neptune denotes imagination and development of a higher intellect, the enrichment that comes through saturating our awareness in symbolism, mythology, and archetypes. Almost every astrologer and mystic I know has Mercury in aspect to Neptune natally. Neptune is the field of the higher Mind that brings inspiration and expanded spiritual perception to the thinking mind. This combination is also seen commonly in the charts of those gifted in poetry and imaginative writing of all kinds, as well as those drawn to the study of religious and metaphysical doctrines. Transits of Neptune to Mercury (or progressed aspects of these two planets) may correspond to periods where it is difficult to focus the mind and our attention may be scattered and impractical. I prefer to utilize these periods for reading and reflection on astrology and esoteric studies, and for losing myself in the imaginative realms of fiction and film. Mercury-Pluto symbolizes investigation and research, persuasive expression of ideas, and allowing our views to be influenced by the ideas of others. During a transit of Pluto conjunct his Mercury-Neptune in Sagittarius a man gave his first lectures as a professor of English literature at an Ivy League university. A woman named Freida having the identical transit was receiving training by a spiritual teacher who was deeply imprinting his ideas upon her. Reinhold Ebertin notes that Mercury-Pluto contacts are associated with "good powers of observation, . . . the wielding of influence through speaking and writing, . . . the power to influence the public or the masses, successes as speaker or writer."[18] Following the transiting and progressed aspects involving Mercury enables us to understand the many ways in which the powers of our intelligence can be focused and expressed.

Venus

Venus governs our evolution as beings of the heart, able to connect with others, to give and receive love and affection. Venus also represents refined tastes and appreciation of whatever is beautiful, refined, and pleasingly formed. When Liz (Chart #5) had progressed Sun conjunct natal Venus she became very artistic, drawing elaborate mandala designs. A woman named Betty had transiting Saturn conjunct natal Venus in Aries in her 4th house. She bought a house with her boyfriend, and she was so happy because it felt great to make a commitment to the relationship (Saturn conjunct Venus), and she just loved fixing up her home (Venus in 4th). Venus was the focus of her evolutionary path at that time.

A 16-year-old young woman with transiting Pluto conjunct natal Venus in her 5th house developed a loving relationship with her first boyfriend, only to have their feelings change when they both flirted with other people, evoking intense jealousy. She learned important lessons about what a powerful, precious, and delicate thing love is.

Astrological studies teach us important lessons that can expand our capacity to love. First and foremost, we can use our charts to solve the Venus-Mars riddle of how to meet our basic needs for companionship and erotic love. We become aware that we are more likely to experience new relationships (or heightened sense of closeness within an existing relationships) during transits of Mars, Jupiter, Saturn, Uranus, or Pluto to natal Venus, or the Venus-Mars midpoint; or transits of these planets into the 7th house. Especially important are stationary retrograde or stationary direct periods of transiting planets in aspect to Venus or the Venus-Mars midpoint, or in the 7th house. Aspects of the progressed Sun or Moon to Venus and Mars are also significant, as well as transits or progressed aspects to natal planets in the 7th house. Other planetary symbols for finding new love and forming new relationships include progressed Sun conjunct, semisquare, or square Venus; progressed Sun-Venus conjunction; progressed Venus-Mars in any major aspect; solar arc Mars conjunct, semisquare, square, sesquiquadrate, or opposite Venus; and (in some cases) progressed Sun aspecting the ruler of the 7th house.

Astrology not only suggests when new relationships may begin, it also helps us sustain our relationships over time. We learn to go through life's changes together, with awareness of planetary cycles, seeing the ever-changing pattern of the sky reflected in the changing moods and feelings of the relationship. We note correlations between transiting interplanetary aspects and the interpersonal climate of the moment. We observe, for example, that when the transiting Moon is in aspect to Mars we might experience a burst of energy, or an irritable mood; or when the Moon is aspecting Saturn we find ourselves focused on our work and responsibilities. We sense that a relationship is not permanently and irrevocably flawed if there are periodic moments of discord, or boredom with one another. This is inevitable, even in the most loving relationships. We begin to accept the changing moods and rhythms of our loved one (as well as our own), and we see how the other person's life direction or current tasks may be different from our own. In *Therapeutic Astrology*, I wrote, "Astrology can teach us to travel through life with another person allowing the periods of lusty passion and delight to ebb and flow, to come and go like the tides coming in and going out, never being attached to one experience at the expense of another."[19]

To make any relationship work we need patience, ceaseless striving to communicate more clearly with one another, and tolerance of imperfections. Aspects between Venus and Saturn are opportunities to learn the lessons of acceptance, not judging the other person's path. As the Hawaiian Huna teachings say, "To love is to be happy with." Natal Venus-Saturn aspects, transiting Saturn aspecting Venus, or progressed Venus aspecting Saturn evoke the theme of learning to love a real person, to accept both the goodness and the limitations of one's friend, lover, or spouse. We begin to accept the divine imperfection of the beloved. Venus-Saturn aspects ask us to grow up, face our unrealistic expectations, and accept the humanity of our partners. We build a sense of trust, loyalty, and enduring commitment. A woman named Kate had the progressed Sun pass over her natal Venus-Saturn opposition (Chart #6). After years of romantic disappointment, Kate learned to accept a real and flawed man—a good, reliable person whom at first she thought wasn't intellectually exciting enough for her, but whom eventually she came to love and value for his good character and loyalty.

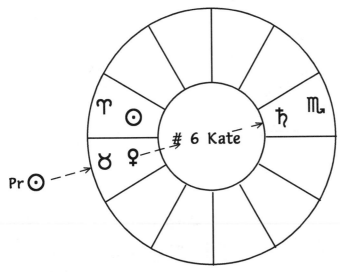

Saturn contacts with Venus often highlight the issue of commitment. Angelica had dated Ed for six months. When transiting Saturn formed the first of three squares to her natal Venus, Angelica asked Ed whether he felt he was committed to their relationship. Ed panicked and withdrew, avoiding speaking to her for a week. This led to several rocky weeks during which their relationship was on hold, Ed stating that he thought maybe he should date other people. As transiting Saturn turned retrograde Ed started pursuing Angelica quite actively again. She pulled back, saying she wasn't sure she could trust him. As Saturn turned direct in motion they started seeing each other again seriously. They both felt they were right for each other. By the time of the last Saturn square Venus they got engaged. The transit corresponded to a lengthy process of facing fears, exploring their alternatives, and then freely choosing to direct their affection toward one another.

A 51-year-old woman named Roberta with transiting Saturn opposing her natal Sun-Venus conjunction in Sagittarius expressed deep maturity in relationship (Chart #7). She agreed to allow John, her husband, who was eight years younger than she, to separate so he could have children with a younger woman, to whom he became magnetically attracted when transiting Pluto squared *his* natal Venus in his 5th house (children). Roberta loved John so much that she only wanted his happiness, and she was willing to

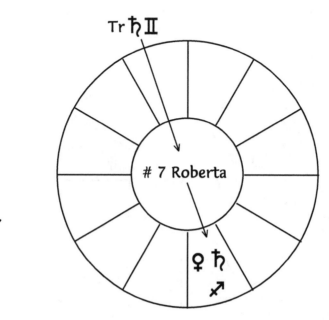

Tr ♄ ♊

7 Roberta

♀ ♄ ♐

7

let go of him if it meant he would have a chance to find greater happiness. The fact that this occurred during a Saturn transit was significant. A purely event-oriented approach to astrology might only see in this a misfortune or potential suffering for Roberta. But from her standpoint this decision was a conscious choice, one she felt she could live with. It was the path of integrity and truth for everybody. Roberta soon remarried.

Natal, transiting, or progressed aspects between Venus and Uranus emphasize freedom in love, instant attraction, sudden changes in love; ambivalence and coolness within a relationship; and freedom to define relationships according to new models. Uranian relationships may be those in which partners encourage each other's individuality and prefer a lot of distance and independence. Or one of the partners may be very funny, unusual, idiosyncratic, or unique. Venus-Uranus may indicate nontraditional relationships—for example, with someone from a different ethnic or social background, or a person much older or younger than ourselves.

Theresa married a man seventeen years younger than her while transiting Uranus was conjunct her natal Venus. Another woman, Ellen, broke up with her longtime boyfriend and began seeing two men simultaneously under the transit of Uranus conjunct natal Venus in Aquarius.

Cheryl had Venus conjunct Sun in Aquarius and Uranus in her 7th house. She got involved with a man who refused to be tied down and would make no commitment. Their relationship was very free, very tumultuous; and while it did not conform to cultural norms and ideals of marriage, commitment, and fidelity, Cheryl felt it was deeply transformative for her to love this man. They got together somewhat irregularly and unpredictably and gave each other plenty of space to be independent and have other friends.

Amy got involved with another woman for the first time when solar arc Uranus squared her natal Venus. She was very freaked out when this happened, but she allowed this relationship to unfold because they had excellent communication and were very compatible.

Venus-Pluto aspects (natally or by transit or progression) often signify themes of deep erotic fascination or obsession, jealousy, betrayal, or issues of control in relationships. Venus-Pluto aspects may signify profoundly magnetic attractions. A man with transiting Pluto square Venus got involved in the most sexually juicy, erotic relationship he had experienced in over thirty years. He said, "I can't believe the things we are doing in bed together." Ellen, with progressed Venus closely squaring natal and progressed Pluto, was having an affair with a married man. She learned that sometimes forbidden love is quite powerful and unforgettable, but also tragic and fraught with complications.

A woman named Joyce had a Venus-Pluto conjunction in the 7th house. She has had two marriages featuring betrayals and triangles, hostility and rage, followed by divorce. Her flirtations and extra- curricular relationships with other men elicited feelings of seething jealousy and acts of vengeful reprisal by both of her husbands. She has been unconscious of this dynamic and keeps playing it out compulsively. She is currently in therapy examining why she repeats these patterns, defiling the beauty and purity of love, and inflicting great pain on herself and others.

Gerard, a jazz musician, had transiting Pluto conjunct his natal Venus. He fell madly in love with his wife of nine years, writing compositions inspired by her. He exuded happiness and contentment when performing on stage. He was absorbed with his feelings of love and attraction, and turned these feelings into inspired expression of his musical gifts.

Most of us are very focused on our search for Venus-Mars love, erotic, passionate, sexual love. Without this, we sometimes experience deep sadness. For some years I have counseled a teacher of Tantra who crashes into severe depression whenever she doesn't have a lover. There is no joy, no happiness in her heart at such times, yet she presents herself to the public as a very evolved, enlightened yogini. Her freedom is utterly conditional. Astrology teaches the lesson that desire (Venus-Mars love) is only one facet of love. The wise person lives the moment of desire fully, without becoming fixated on it.

Astrological studies can expand our capacity to love by teaching us to express a broader spectrum of love. For example, Venus-Neptune aspects may teach us lessons of selfless, unconditional love. A young woman with natal Venus-Neptune conjunct in the 7th house was married to a man who became disabled and required constant care. Her path of spiritual evolution required learning selfless service to her husband. Natal, transiting, or progressed contacts of Venus-Neptune are among the most expansive astrological influences, symbolizing adoration of our loved ones, devotional love, love directed toward God/Goddess, Spirit, the Absolute. We see

Venus-Neptune aspects in the charts of people drawn to the path of divine love and opening the heart through devotional yoga, chanting, and spiritual attunement through music and sacred sound. Ammachi, a woman saint from India whom many consider an *avatar* of divine love, has natal Venus opposite Neptune; she teaches ecstatic chanting of the divine name. Musician George Harrison had Venus in the 5th house (performance and creativity) in the final degree of Pisces, opposite Neptune; his songs were a joyous expression of love and spiritual devotion. Venus in its highest expression represents the power of love to join us together, to make peace, to heal the world.

Mars

Mars symbolizes our animal needs for physical movement and release of energy through expression of our drives, desires, passion, anger, and vitality. Attention to the planet Mars in our birth charts and transits teaches us about the optimal expression of our life force. Sometimes we need to activate our vitality through physical activity and exertion. While transiting Uranus was square natal Mars, a woman felt an intense internal heat and burned off twenty pounds through vigorous exercise. A client named Melanie with progressed Sun square Mars became quite combative; she was obsessed with karate and weightlifting, and had several disputes at home, at work, with other motorists on the road. She had become direct, blunt, and assertive. She said, "I am very into my body lately; I feel like a wild, fierce animal. I cruised a bar the other night and took a guy home, totally out of character. What is happening to me? And why am I fighting with everyone? And why can't I meditate?" Melanie's wholeness of being requires integration of Mars, which is the energy-impulse to go directly after what we want.

During Mars transits we have opportunities to free up our sexual energies, whether we have been repressed about it or overly fixated on it. A 58-year-old woman with transiting Neptune conjunct Mars began exploring how sex and spirituality merged after attending a Tantra workshop in which she felt streams of energy running through her body.

When a former Roman Catholic Priest had transiting Pluto conjunct natal Mars in Scorpio, he had a dream of a wolf sleeping in front of an altar. His associations to this dream image were that he was now a lone wolf who had to hunt, to fend for his own survival without the protection of the Church; and that the wolf represented his long slumbering desire nature, now awakening. The wolf in front of the altar meant that rediscovering his sexuality was sacred; it was associated with a place, and feeling, of worship.

A man with transiting Uranus opposite his natal Mars-Saturn-Pluto conjunction in Leo did extensive psychotherapy to resolve compulsive sexual behaviors emphasizing pain and domination. A client with transiting Pluto square Mars experienced a burning heat at the base of his spine, followed by an awakening of a powerful inner current of energy that rose up to his brain, a classic *kundalini* awakening, a higher evolutionary transmutation of Mars energy.

Invariably, Mars transits heat things up. Some Mars lessons occur through disagreements, clashes, and incidents. A woman with natal Mars in the 4th house came from a very volatile family, which ignited in conflict every time transiting Mars aspected its natal position. During a recent Mars retrograde transit conjunct my natal Mars in the 3rd house of driving and transportation I had several auto mishaps. First I scraped up my car backing into a parking space. Then, while I was picking up a load of manure for my garden, my pickup truck was rammed by a tractor. Then my neighbors (3rd house) brought home a loud barking dog. And on the final pass of Mars conjunct natal Mars I had an accident while kayaking and bruised my ribs (again!). I could hardly breathe. The 3rd house rules the breath! A life of consciousness through astrology includes bearing the tension of these incidents and mishaps.

Don was the target of sexual harassment at work by his male employer while progressed Mars in the 6th house was inconjunct natal Sun (Chart #8). This incident occurred on the day of a new Moon in Virgo conjunct Pluto in his 8th house; sexual abuse in the workplace is symbolized by both 8th house Pluto in Virgo, and progressed Mars in the 6th house (employment). Progressed Mars also completed a Yod pattern involving natal Sun quincunx Pluto.[20] Don came to see me because he was having problems with anger management. He was quite irritable at home, had gotten into a fistfight in a nightclub, and injured himself by kicking a door in a fit of anger, banging up his foot rather nicely. Once he sorted out his feelings about the incident at work and changed jobs he began to feel calmer and less combative.

We can learn to transform our relationship to the Mars principle. A woman with natal Mars in her 4th house (home and family) told me, "My mother

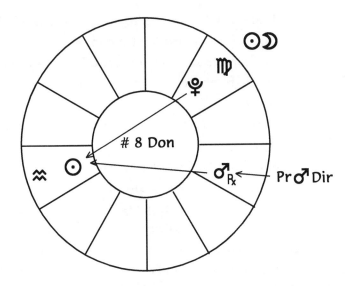

was an enraged, screaming maniac. But my own family household is very harmonious. There is very little screaming. I'm in a very male-oriented environment. I have a male dog, a son who is into martial arts, and my husband is in law enforcement, and he's a very manly, athletic guy. I like this way of living my Mars much better."

At this point I'd like to briefly mention a point of technique. One of the primary methods I use is to follow interplanetary transit cycles, such as the Sun-Mercury cycle and the Jupiter-Saturn cycle, the cycle of social achievement and professional advancement.[21] I also follow Mars in relationship to other planets. Following the transit cycles of Venus-Mars is a key to understanding the cycles of sex, romance, the heat and play of attraction. Periodically Venus and Mars form major aspects to one another such as the conjunction, square, and opposition, and these are times when sexual relationships may intensify. While transiting Mars and Venus were conjunct in Leo, one woman had a very erotic relationship. She said, "I can die content knowing that I have experienced sex like that."

Mars operating in relationship with Jupiter represents increase of vitality and positive activation of the will through enterprise and adventure.[22] Mars-Saturn as a planetary pair denotes intense effort and discipline, self-control, focused expression of energy and desire. Mars-Neptune contacts can manifest as heightened erotic imagination and sensitivity, or as the tendency to dissipate energy through excessive sexual fantasy. Here is an example combining both Mars-Saturn and Mars-Neptune themes: While transiting Saturn opposed his natal Mars-Neptune in Scorpio, a man did intensive psychotherapy to explore his elaborate sexual fantasies and addiction to pornography, and to re-enliven his relationship with his wife. Self-mastery is part of the *raja yoga*.[23]

Mars-Uranus contacts electrify us and ignite our inner fire, and can also manifest through impetuous, obstinate expression of our desires, independence, or individuality. Mars-Neptune aspects correspond to intensified longing to reach our ideals and to attain spiritual freedom; in other instances these contacts manifest through feelings of weakness, or indecisiveness, with Mars amplifying Neptune's passivity or sense of martyrdom. Mars-Neptune can also signify the current of ecstasy. Mars-Pluto aspects symbolize high energy and physical strength, and are found in the charts of many athletes. Also, Mars-Pluto transforms the fire of anger through release of seething fury, destructive use of will, and injurious behaviors; this combination calls for the systematic rooting out of all vestiges of enmity or violence.[24]

We need wisdom to guide our optimal expression of our life energy. What is most important is that we not remain fixated at this level—fixated on anger, sex, or assertion of our will in every situation. The steady, unobstructed flame of Mars energy can fuel our pursuit of every evolutionary goal.

Jupiter

Jupiter represents growth through digesting food, knowledge, and life experience, and through pursuing our highest goals and aspirations. At this level of consciousness we seek truth, wisdom, and expansion through travel, learning, and the company of learned teachers. The natal placement of Jupiter shows us an area of life where our growth is most free and uninhibited. A woman with Jupiter in the 9th house (and trine her Sun) loves to visit other countries. A gardener with a Venus-Jupiter conjunction in the 4th house loves to work in the earth and to cultivate the growth and beauty of plants. Jade, a business consultant with Jupiter in her 2nd house, always earned lots of money.

Transits or progressions involving Jupiter are moments of opportunity when we experience some helpful opening of doors, improvement in some area of life; we are shown the way forward to a better future. Jupiter represents our sense of good fortune as we meet the grace that fulfills our desires. A woman with chronic money problems got a substantial raise when transiting Jupiter passed through her 2nd house; her true worth was validated. A 41-year-old woman became pregnant for the first time when transiting Jupiter was conjunct her 5th house Moon. A schoolteacher named Matt who had been ill for several years and not working asked me, "Are there any signs of luck for me in career?" (This is how many people talk to astrologers.) I noted that transiting Jupiter in Pisces was passing through Matt's 10th house, stationary retrograde squaring natal Jupiter in Sagittarius (Chart #9). There was reason to be optimistic; by all means, he should seek employment immediately! Within two weeks he had several excellent job offers in the field of education (Jupiter in Sagittarius). Jupiter reminds us that there is fullness and opportunity in our world.

Transits of Jupiter are times for us to reach higher, to set new goals, to seek expansion. When transiting Jupiter was conjunct the Midheaven and opposite his natal Moon-Venus-Jupiter in the 4th house, a man built an extension onto his house and created a large space he used for movement, music, meditation, and holding classes. When transiting Jupiter was conjunct natal Mars in her 5th house, a mother's relationship with her son improved dramatically. They began taking *aikido* classes together and formed a shared commitment to peaceful warriorship.

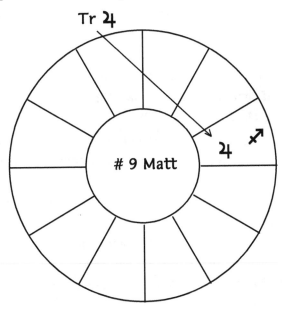

A man with Jupiter in Libra in the 7th house always had many friends. At his Jupiter return (at age 36) he got married to a professor of art (Jupiter in Libra). Through her, he developed friendships with other highly educated people. Each planet represents a certain kind of character in our lives: Saturn is an older person, or an authority figure. Mars is a competitor, a blunt, demanding, or self-assertive person. Moon represents a woman, a nurturing person, a person we care about. Venus is someone very attractive, beautiful, or artistic. Jupiter represents contacts with teachers, people of learning, or highly ethical or principled individuals. Jupiter also symbolizes our relationship to the whole realm of culture, education, ethics, and civilized values.

Jupiter signifies our aspiration to uphold high principles. A woman with Mars-Jupiter conjunct in Sagittarius was fiercely committed to truth and justice and spoke out often on behalf of human rights. At its best, Jupiter brings positive intensity about our convictions. A retired scientist with Jupiter in Aquarius in her 11th house became a leader in the local environmental movement in her county, an outspoken advocate for social change (Aquarius) who developed skills of group organizing and moral leadership (Jupiter in 11th house). Mohandas Gandhi had Jupiter conjunct Pluto in Taurus, opposite Mars-Saturn in Scorpio in the first house. His unshakeable moral convictions had immense power, awakening in others the strength to stand up to a mighty world empire, and causing others to reevaluate the ethics of their own actions (Jupiter-Pluto in 7th). His Jupiter-Pluto stands as an enduring symbol of *satyagraha*, truth force, the expression of power without violence.

Julia Butterfly Hill, who spent two years living in a redwood tree as an act of nonviolent civil disobedience, has Jupiter-Sun conjunct in Aquarius, closely squaring Mars in Taurus. She took a moral stand and carried out an unprecedented action to express her love of the Earth. Her Mars-Jupiter square gives her what one writer called "great tenacity and determined willingness to fight for a cause."[25]

Jupiter's association with morality and strongly held principles is also at the root of our tendency toward intolerance and excessive zeal when we are influenced by this planet. It is the planet of the dogmatist, the proselytizer, the moralist. In contrast, an underdeveloped Jupiter can manifest as poor judgement rooted in a weak internal code of conduct. My friend Shelley

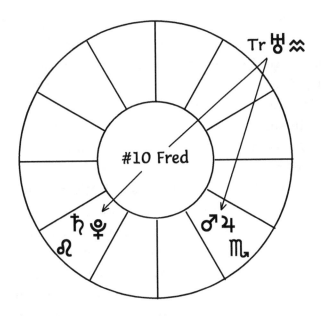

Jordan told me the story of a successful business entrepreneur with natal Jupiter in Virgo conjunct his Ascendant, trine his Moon in Taurus in the 9th house. "At his age 36 Jupiter return he was convicted of fraud and the story was all over the local newspapers. He had what most astrologers would call a prominent Jupiter. But the planets only reflect back your internal constructs. This man didn't have adequate ethics, deep-seated morality, or strongly held principles. That's what got him in trouble."[26]

The shadow of Jupiter also includes laziness, blind optimism, gluttony, excess, going to extremes. A woman who deeply loves her family exhausted herself with excessive caretaking, house-cleaning, and Christmas shopping, when transiting Jupiter was conjunct her Cancer Moon. She said, "I always overdo it." A man named Fred with Mars-Jupiter conjunct in the 5th house enjoyed card games and gambling (Chart #10). However, he also had Saturn-Pluto in the 2nd house; and when transiting Uranus opposed Saturn-Pluto his luck ran out on him, leaving him with some large debts. True to the character of Jupiter, Fred accepted this downturn in his fortunes cheerfully, and optimistically planned his next trip to Las Vegas.

More typically, attunement to Jupiter manifests as an urge to try something a little extravagant, to eat a little more, or buy some new clothes, or spend a little more money on a business card to make it look really snazzy; or we take a chance on love, revealing ourselves more authentically and openly to others. Jupiter also signifies trust in destiny, faith in the future; we trust that things will work out for the best. But Jupiter's traditional association with luck and good fortune only holds true if we make the right effort. A passive hopefulness will yield poor results. Responsiveness to Jupiter means that we *act* on moments of opportunity, seizing every chance available to us for growth and expansion. In other words, Jupiter's planning and goal-setting needs to be linked to Mars' energy and initiative, and Saturn's focus and sustained commitment.

When we have taken positive steps to better ourselves or develop our work in life, Jupiter sometimes manifests as specific awards or recognition of our accomplishments. Jim graduated from Massage School and began a successful practice when transiting Jupiter was conjunct his Ascendant, square Mars-Saturn in the 10th house. A writer had his first spy novel published and received favorable reviews when transiting Jupiter, ruler of his Sagittarius MC, was conjunct natal Sun-Mercury-Neptune in Scorpio in his 9th house. A woman received a major promotion to a corporate management position when transiting Jupiter was conjunct her Sun-Pluto in the 10th house. Rabindranath Tagore won the 1913 Nobel Prize for literature with transiting Jupiter conjunct his Midheaven.

Terrence McKenna was born with Jupiter in the 12th house conjunct his Scorpio Sun.[27] He was an intrepid explorer of visionary consciousness and the inner worlds (12th house) who went on exotic voyages (Jupiter) to South America in search of shamans and their potent brews. McKenna enjoyed his period of greatest recognition in the early 1990s while transiting Jupiter was conjunct his MC. He also had progressed Sun sextile Jupiter; solar arc Jupiter semisquare Jupiter; solar arc Neptune conjunct Sun-Venus; and transiting Pluto conjunct natal Sun-Venus. He enjoyed enormous popularity and influence for several years, developing a unique mix of ethnobotany, witty social commentary, apocalyptic mysticism, and speculation on physics, cyberspace, and the shape of Time. He exemplified Jupiterian qualities of adventurous spirit, hunger for knowledge, and propensity for concept-building and expansive philosophical expression. McKenna's life was a fast-burning supernova.[28]

Jupiter symbolizes intellectual pursuits, regardless of whether or not this occurs within formal educational institutions. I taught my first astrology classes at my age 24 Jupiter return. I began teaching in universities when transiting Uranus squared natal Jupiter, and when transiting Saturn opposed natal Jupiter. Jupiter, through its rulership of Sagittarius, represents our involvement with all processes of teaching, instruction, and tutelage—both as a student, receiving knowledge with eager receptivity, and teaching others, skillfully conveying our knowledge to others. When transiting Jupiter was conjunct his natal Jupiter-Neptune in Sagittarius, a man received advanced instruction in the philosophy and practice of Tibetan Vajrayana Buddhism.

Jupiter is the planet of great teachers. Philosopher-sage Sri Aurobindo had a Sun-Jupiter conjunction in Leo, denoting his majestic presence and vast knowledge. To read his words is to directly encounter his refined consciousness. Jupiter also represents our ability to access the *inner* teacher, our inner wisdom and knowing. We learn to rely on the inner *guru* and its mysterious guidance. Aurobindo described this process in a passage I will cite at length below, in the section on Neptune. But at some stages of our journeys we are inspired by the words and living presence of the embodied Teacher.

Jupiter is a focal point in my own chart, and I have spent a lot of time seeking out teachers. When I was fourteen years old I met Muni Chitrabanu, a Jain yogi who had spent years meditating and observing a lengthy vow of silence; he was an emanation of love. I studied meditation with Swami Muktananda for eight years, and received intensive instruction from my *hatha yoga* gurus, Allan Bateman and Judith Lasater. When transiting Saturn was conjunct natal Jupiter, I spent several months in Chicago attending lectures by the brilliant philosopher, Paul Ricoeur. Another influential teacher was David Spangler, born with Jupiter conjunct Neptune in Libra, a mystic and visionary who accesses deep inner wisdom during his lucid, inspiring lectures. Later I studied with Stanley Krippner (born with Jupiter-Neptune conjunct in Virgo), a pre-eminent scholar of dreams, parapsychology, states of consciousness, and cross-cultural healing modalities.

When transiting Jupiter was square natal Mercury, and solar arc Mercury closely squared my natal Jupiter (also, my progressed Moon was in Sagittarius), I showed up on the doorstep of my astrology teacher, Andrés Takra, who, in his kindness, offered to pay me to assist him with his research. Each day I would sit with him while he instructed me. I wrote down everything he taught me.[29] I'll never forget my first lesson. He told me, "Astrology is a sacred and solemn science. It can enlighten you, or it can make you crazy. It can paralyze your free will, or it can make you a bold, successful, evolved human being. It is up to you." Everything that I have attempted to do in the field of astrology can be seen as an outgrowth of that lesson. Takra's Jupiter precisely opposed my Sun. He himself is a Jupiterian figure with Jupiter conjunct Pluto in Leo, square Mars. A scholar and world traveler, Andrés had served as Venezuelan ambassador to India (Jupiter: international affairs), stationed for several years in New Delhi, where he hobnobbed with all the local yogis and *jyotishas* (astrologers). He had a vast library full of rare books on astrology, yoga, and mysticism, which I devoured hungrily. We would spend days at a time hunkering down in the library of his opulent home in Boulder, Colorado, reading and discussing books on topics such as *vimsottari dasa* progressions in Hindu astrology, the history and mythology of the sidereal zodiac (especially Cyril Fagan's *Astrological Origins*[30]), and how to rectify a birth time by examining the shape of a person's face. He fed me protein drinks and drove me around in his red Jaguar. With a 5th house Cancer Sun, Takra is a man of ease, comfort, and infectious warmth, with many children, a great mentor. I was so blessed to have spent this time with him.

There are many ways we can relate to teachers. We spend time with them, going to them for instruction.[31] Just being in the presence of a man or woman of wisdom uplifts us. We contemplate their words and actions. We consider who they are, what their lives means to us. We write to them, posing our questions, and perhaps receive back some helpful words of guidance. I had the chance to correspond with Dane Rudhyar near the end of his life, while transiting Saturn was aspecting my natal Jupiter. In one letter, Rudhyar wrote,

> Yes, being "in" the world but not "of" it is very difficult. It is man's supreme power that he can live consistently at more than one or two levels. Polyphonic, counterpunctual living—Caesar *and* God (say the Gospels). Yet there are periods when singleness of purpose and an all-absorbing focus of vision are required to move safely through the rite of passage. Keep on with your work and do not be impatient if the field of transhuman activity and consciousness seems enveloped in mist. Clarity comes only most gradually, and one

has to build means of formulation that emerge out of one's own experiences, indeed out of crises courageously and nobly passed through.

Rudhyar's phrase "polyphonic, counterpunctual living" has inspired me greatly as I consider how to live harmoniously on many levels of existence concurrently. We have to live in the world and fulfill our responsibilities while also seeking a life of expanded consciousness and spiritual freedom. Also, Rudhyar is saying that we have to figure things out for ourselves. A teacher can point the way, but as astrologers we must pass through our own consciously lived experiences and find meaning in them. We see, with awe, that our lives are unfolding according to coherent structural principles. Rudhyar's words are as potent for me today as they were the day I received his letter in 1984.

Over two decades ago, when transiting Jupiter was conjunct my Midheaven, and my progressed Moon was conjunct natal Jupiter, I traveled to India to see my meditation teacher, Swami Muktananda. He gazed into my eyes, bestowing his blessing. I had several moments alone with him: our souls touched. I practiced *guru yoga*, inner identification with the teacher's enlightened consciousness. I saw the infinity of space and the brightness of galaxies in his eyes. The mantra *So'Ham* reverberated inside me with the powerful resonance of eternal Being. These practices propelled me into an expanded state of consciousness lasting several weeks. I was pulled from within into the heart of deep meditation. My breath became very subtle; the mind was completely still, in union with Source. All awareness of duality dissolved into blissful awareness of pure consciousness. I perceived the constant throbbing and expansive pulsation of consciousness in all creation. Being in the company of someone established in an expanded state enabled me to glimpse a more evolved condition.[32]

Some teachers play a role in our lives through story, legend, and written records of their words. Indian guru Shirdi Sai Baba (1838–1918) was born with a Sun-Jupiter conjunction in Libra.[33] He was a benevolent source of wisdom, solace, and blessing to all who sought him out. Every word he uttered was Truth. He was also renowned as a healer who used herbal remedies to cure the ailments of others. He slept on a narrow plank inside a dilapidated mosque, and could often be found tending the flame of a seemingly eternal fire. His teachings include the following statements:

Action: This present fate is the result of the *karma* (action) done by you in former births.

Charity: The donor gives, that is sows his seeds, only to reap a rich harvest in the future. Wealth should be the means to work out *dharma*. If it is not given before, you do not get it now. So, the best way to receive is to give.

Death: None dies; see with your inner eyes. Then you will realize that you are God and not different from Him. Like wornout garments the body is cast away.

Duty: Unless a [person] discharges satisfactorily and disinterestedly the duties of his [or her] station in life, his [or her] mind will not be purified.

Equanimity: Let the world go topsy-turvy, you remain where you are. Standing or staying at your own place, look calmly at the show of all things passing before you.

God's Grace: Always adhere to truth and fulfill all the promises you make. Have faith and patience. Then God will always be with you wherever you are.

Goodness: If you act in a good way, good will really follow.

Hospitality: No one comes to us without *rinanubandha* (past karmic bonds). So when any dog, cat, pig, fly or person approaches you, do not drive it or him away.

Humility: Humility is not toward all. Severity is necessary in dealing with the wicked.

All the world is full of pulls or problems, you keep on your path. Remain unmoved by the curiosity; remain detached. As you sow, so shall you reap. As are one's motives, so are the results of one's actions. Your actions go with you. Others' actions go with them. Do not compete with anyone else. Do not speak ill of anyone else.

It is not essential that one have a Guru. Everything is within us. What you sow, so you reap. What you give, you get. There is no need for a Guru. It is all within you. Try to listen within and follow the direction you get.[34]

The inspiring teachings and expansive experiences we receive from teachers must be tested and practiced in our daily lives. We need to bring an enlightened consciousness to a variety of life situations. The wisdom and uplifted attitude symbolized by Jupiter take root inside us as we learn to access the ground of clarity within, remember who we really are, and abide in the Light of Awareness, even in our moments of greatest difficulty. Recently somebody with progressed Sun square Mars got quite angry with me. I found it somewhat uncomfortable to be screamed at, and initially I tried to argue with this person. Then some deeper part of me emerged and I tried to calm down and bring my inner center of wisdom and understanding to the situation. I saw that the other person needed to be angry in that moment, and

I could listen and allow this. Eventually the other person was able to stop yelling and explain to me some points I had not fully understood. We ended up having a reasonable and principled interaction filled with mutual respect and understanding. We were able to reach a place where we both perceived the inner light of divinity in one another. This experience occurred when solar arc Jupiter was exactly semisquare my natal Sun. Jupiter teaches us that patience, tolerance, and a forgiving attitude can enhance our quality of life.

Jupiter signifies the formation of a belief system, principles to live by. For example, I try to follow these seven teachings from the Hawaiian Huna philosophy:

> *Ike*: The world is what you think it is.
> *Kala*: There are no limits.
> *Makia*: Energy flows where attention goes.
> *Manawa*: Now is the moment of power.
> *Aloha*: To love is to be happy with.
> *Mana*: All power comes from within.
> *Pono*: Effectiveness is the measure of truth.

I often apply these principles to the practice of astrology. For example, reflection on transits and progressions often brings to mind the idea that "Now is the moment of power." We have to find the right course of action or focus of our energies in each moment. We are *conditioned* by the past but not *limited* by it. *Now* is the moment when we can shape the future. There are no limits to what can unfold; the future is an open road.

To further understand the important role of Jupiter, we need to study its rhythmic interplay with Saturn. Each astrologer, and each client who comes to us, can receive great benefit from careful study of the inter-related transit cycles of Jupiter and Saturn—described in Appendix B. Jupiter-Saturn symbolizes steady progress toward tangible goals. I also pay close attention to Jupiter's pairing with the outer planets: Jupiter-Uranus as a planetary pair signifies growth through invention, innovation, breakthroughs, and moments of liberation. Jupiter-Neptune represents growth through assimilation of the principles of religion, spirituality, and metaphysical knowledge. Jupiter-Pluto suggests growth through positive expression of power and influence in the world.

Jupiter's 12-year transit cycle means that this expansive planet frequently forms potent aspects to all our natal planets, giving us new chances to awaken our potentials. Hope and growth spring eternal. Jupiter's abiding presence in our lives affirms an endless horizon of possibilities.

Saturn

One of our major evolutionary tasks is to actualize our aspirations and goals through disciplined and sustained effort. These are the lessons of Saturn. Here we fulfill the requirements of life within form, within the structures, responsibilities, and commitments that give our lives focus and stability. We build the edifice of our lives one piece at a time. Inayat Khan said, "Love climbs the mountains of life, step by step."[35] Those who are having difficulty with a Saturn transit need to get grounded and adjust better to the requirements of living in a body, in the material and social realms. 90% of my astrological work involves helping people at the level of Saturn, with problems of social adaptation, career choice, material struggles, and maturational challenges. This is crucial for all of us, because without resilient structures we founder. If someone who is lost seeks direction through astrology, he or she can find it by locating the natal and current transiting positions of Saturn. These instruct us about where in our lives we need to work hard to build greater stability. Our goal here is to become well adapted, to live more or less comfortably within our societal-cultural environment. Saturn, with its regular and unceasing transit cycle, makes repeated, cyclic visitations, presenting us with a series of lessons of practicality, maturity, and stability. Saturn forms a major aspect to its natal position every seven or eight years. These constitute a progressive series of lessons that always refer to Saturn's natal house and sign placement, as well as transiting Saturn's current house and sign placement.

For example, someone who has natal Saturn in the 7th house might have significant issues regarding marriage and partnership at each stage of the Saturn cycle. A woman named Beth (Chart #11), with Saturn in the 7th married and established a household at age 21 (Saturn 3/4 square), and had two children during her Saturn return (Saturn in Leo), deepening her marital

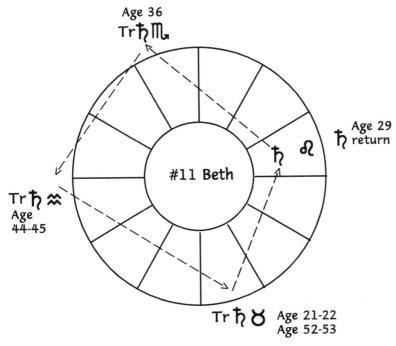

commitment. At age 36 (Saturn 1/4 square), while Saturn passed through her 10th house of career, she went back to work and started building a new career. This caused some conflict in her marriage because she had less time to spend with her husband (Saturn square Saturn in the 7th house). At the Saturn opposition (Saturn in her 1st house) she had important decisions to make with her husband about one of their children, who had academic problems (natal Saturn in Leo; transiting Saturn in 1st house, which is the education 9th house from the child 5th house). They had to be responsible adults together. At her 3/4 square of Saturn (in Taurus) Beth's children left home and went to college. She and her husband sold their home and purchased a new one in another city (transiting Saturn in 4th house). Just from tracing the Saturn cycle you can see the outline of some major events in Beth's life: marriage, giving birth, new career and success, responsibilities and decisions regarding children, launching young adults, a happy empty nest, and relocation. It is the same for all of us. Our lives unfold on schedule following the rhythms of the Saturn cycle.[36]

In some instances a person will struggle with the lessons of Saturn, the lessons of maturity. Consider the story of Ted (Chart #12), who has Saturn-Neptune in Libra in the 8th house: At his first Saturn return, Ted got married.

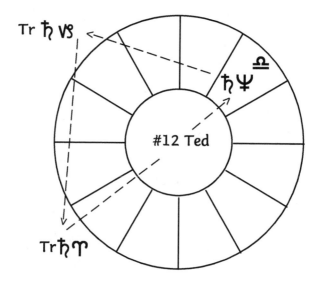

He couldn't find a job and fell into a pattern of drinking and drug use (Saturn conjunct Neptune). By the time of his first quarter Saturn square at age 36, he had become a full-blown alcoholic and cocaine addict. Then during his Saturn opposition in his mid forties, he got divorced (Saturn in the 8th house). The harsh reality of alimony and child support forced a major self-assessment that led to his cleaning up, going through detox, getting a regular job. Transiting Saturn was in the 2nd house of money opposite 8th house Saturn: shared finances, financial obligations to others. These became the new structures and responsibilities of his life. Ted did not cope well with reality during his Saturn return. So fifteen years later, at the Saturn opposition, he was forced to grow up and come down to earth. This example also illustrates a basic principle of Dane Rudhyar's philosophy—that cycles are unceasing, and that even if we fail to achieve all the goals of a particular cycle, the compassion of Being always provides another opportunity to complete the unfinished evolutionary business of the past.[37] Astrology instills faith in our ultimate ability to achieve our evolutionary goals, because even where we have faced obstacles or failures we trust in the unfolding of new cycles in the future.

I'd like to tell you a story that illustrates transition from Saturn-bound consciousness to the level of Uranus and Neptune. A psychiatrist named Sam was divorced and had suffered from severe depression for the past eight years (Chart #13). During this eight-year period his progressed Sun

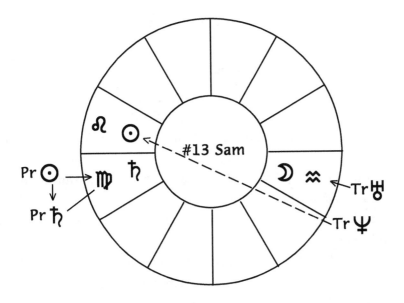

had been conjunct natal and progressed Saturn in Virgo. He was in a state of severe burnout, with many heavy responsibilities as the staff psychiatrist at three hospitals. His life was all work and no play. He presented himself to me as a person utterly without joy; he did not exercise or take care of his health (Saturn in Virgo). It was reassuring to Sam to learn how closely his experience conformed to the archetypal qualities of Saturn. With Saturn in the 1st house, Sam is a father, a man with responsibilities, who has to work. He has learned well the lessons of Saturn and is carrying out his responsibilities nobly. But he has lost touch with his natural joy and sense of play (Leo Sun). His soul seems heavy and fatigued. He is over-identified with his persona, his work role, his social identity as a psychiatrist (Saturn in 1st house). Sam reminds me of the archetypal figure of the wounded King. According to Jungian analyst Marie Louise Von Franz,

> The actual process of individuation—the conscious coming-to-terms with one's own inner center or Self—generally begins with a wounding of the personality and the suffering that accompanies it. . . Many myths and fairy tales symbolically describe this initial stage in the process of individuation by telling of a king who has fallen ill or grown old. Other familiar story patterns are that a royal couple is barren; or that a monster steals all the women, children, horses, and wealth of the kingdom; . . . or that darkness hangs over the lands, wells dry up, and flood, drought, and frost afflict the country. In myths. . . the magic or talisman that can cure the misfortune of

the king or his country always proves to be something very special. In one tale, "a white blackbird" or "a fish that carries a golden ring in its gills" is needed to restore the king's health. In another, the king wants "the waters of life" or "three golden hairs from the head of the devil. . . ." Whatever it is, the thing that can drive away the evil is always unique and hard to find. It is exactly the same in the initial crisis in the life of an individual.[38]

The precious and rare object that must be found to restore king and kingdom to health symbolizes our need to individuate, to live the fullness of who we are. As Von Franz puts it, "The goal of individuation is the realization of the uniqueness of the individual man or woman, so that our inborn possibilities become conscious and we act to bring it into reality."[39] And this is where Uranus and Neptune enter the picture.

Sam had transiting Uranus conjunct his Aquarius Moon in the 6th house. Meditation on this transit brought two insights: He wanted to change jobs, and he also wanted to change his attitude toward his work, to become more of an innovator and change agent at work. He said, "All I do is dispense meds." I suggested that perhaps it was time to get training in some new therapy techniques (6th house Moon). He readily agreed. He said that he wanted to quit working at one job and to work in new ways with some of his patients at another hospital; he was also about to begin working with Native Americans on a reservation. Transiting Uranus conjunct Moon suggested the importance of breaking old patterns in other areas, such as opening up his feelings, finding new modes of self-care, improving his diet (Moon in 6th), learning to cook for himself. Activation of the Moon always raises the issue of how we can take better care of ourselves. This Uranus transit showed the possibility of dramatic personal change. It was a call to Sam to move through his inertia and despair into new freedom.

Transiting Neptune was also beginning a long opposition to his natal Sun, which was placed in Leo in the 12th house. Sam needed to rediscover his spirituality, his interests in meditation, astrology, and metaphysics, which had been strong twenty years earlier. During the lengthy, post-divorce testing of progressed Sun conjunct Saturn in Virgo, Sam had become dry, hardened, depressed, cynical, and dissatisfied. With Neptune opposite natal Sun, it was a time for him to rediscover his sense of awe, mystery, and his original reason for becoming a psychiatrist: to help people. I suggested that he develop an attitude of surrender and self-consecration and desire to serve humanity. At that point, Sam began to cry and for about ten minutes we hardly spoke as he melted down, remembering his original, pure intention. Transiting Jupiter was soon going to be conjunct Sam's natal Venus in the 11th house, which suggested he could begin to connect with people in groups. Also, with transiting Neptune opposite his 12th house Sun, it seemed like a good time to go on a spiritual retreat, to practice meditation.

Three months later I heard back from Sam. He had implemented many of the changes we had discussed and was feeling much happier. He had been dating a woman (transiting Jupiter conjunct Venus, improved social life), and was attending a regular meditation group after going on a weekend retreat that provided some needed peace and spiritual renewal. He had received training in expressive arts and psychodrama techniques that he was using with patients at the hospital (Leo Sun in 12th). He also developed a friendship with a Native American medicine man who became a mentor to him (transiting Uranus and Neptune in the 6th house of training and apprenticeship). He was going in a completely new direction. He commented on the unique power astrology has to assist the healing process. Coming from a psychiatrist, I considered this a statement of considerable importance.

Uranus

Sam's story illustrates positive response to Uranus, the principle of change, metamorphosis. Uranus represents our urge to rebel and experiment, to break free of the past, to pursue unconventional goals, to express our uniqueness. Under the influence of Uranus we become harbingers of changes about to emerge in the collective, like lightning rods of Spirit. Sam began practicing what he called the psychiatry of the future, combining the modern pharmacology and psychotherapy techiques with ancient shamanic, spiritual healing arts.

Jane, a mother and housewife from a remote rural area, consulted with me about her personal metamorphosis (Chart #14). Transiting Uranus was conjunct natal Mercury and square Neptune in Jane's 1st house. She was studying metaphysics and had a gift not only for understanding spiritual teachings but also for communicating them (Mercury square Neptune) to others. She began to lead Church groups in her community, teaching 12-Step principles, meditation, prayer, and visualization. She had also developed

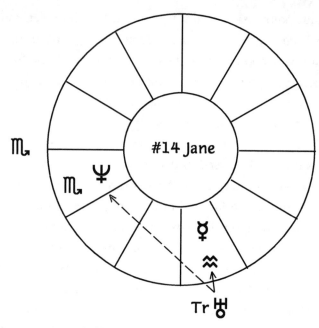

some clairvoyance and did helpful readings for others. Jane lived in a very conservative community, yet people were flocking to hear her discourses. She took her small town by storm, becoming an inspiring spiritual teacher. Dazzling light may be released through any person responding to Uranus. We become change agents, expressing new ideas, inventions, and discoveries that may one day be more widely accepted by the mainstream culture (symbolized by Saturn). We lead the way into the future.

If Saturn symbolizes the reality principle, our need to accept the limits of the world, then Uranus is the principle of invention and novelty, the capacity to reshape reality. Challenging convention and our conditioned perceptions of what is possible, we feel an irresistible excitement about a new interest or pursuit; and we often exhibit a kind of zealous dedication to this project. Do you remember being convinced that a particular new diet or health product or enlightenment course was going to revolutionize the world?

During transits and progressions involving Uranus our lives take new and unexpected turns. We get involved with new activities that may seem radical or strange, but that are later seen as revolutionary or cutting edge. Nancy, a nurse with transiting Uranus conjunct her Midheaven, was introduced to products that use the subtle energy of magnets to alleviate musculo-skeletal imbalances such as spinal misalignments, and for circulatory problems. The magnets also appeared to be effective in alleviating carpal tunnel syndrome, which afflicts thousands of people. Nancy believed that this technology could radically impact health care. She became a distributor of these products and changed her career entirely within the space of a month (Uranus: rapid change). She began selling these magnets to doctors and chiropractors who were open to new alternatives. The culture is ready for change, and those who are aligned with Uranus can become agents of social transformation.

Under the major Uranus visitations (for example, transiting Uranus aspecting the Sun, Moon, or other personal planets, or crossing an angle of the chart), we are ready to embrace major life change. A man passing through his Uranus opposition suddenly decided to quit his job to pursue his lifelong dream of becoming a painter. A woman who had progressed Venus square Uranus suddenly announced to her husband and two children that she was in love with another woman and that she was moving out to buy a house with her. Such is the shocking nature of Uranus. When Uranian lightning strikes, we are seized by a desire to set ourselves free and live according to the true law of our own being. Uranus is the planet of individuation and self-liberating choices.

Technically speaking, it is not accurate to say there is just one planet of individuation, because individuation really means living the whole natal chart. But Uranus gives us specific prods to go beyond social standards, to pursue new directions of thought, lifestyle, or career. When transiting Uranus was conjunct my Sun I wrote and published the book, *Therapeutic Astrology*, describing my personal synthesis of astrology and depth psychotherapy. I am convinced that this is the wave of the future.

Just as with Saturn, we follow the major phases of the Uranus cycle, especially the opening square, opposition, closing square, and the Uranus return at age 84. The Uranus square around age 21 is a crucial time for establishing one's own independent objectives, free of parental and cultural conditioning. During my Uranus square I became an astrologer and a committed practitioner of meditation. Uranus squares Neptune in my natal chart so transiting Uranus was conjunct Neptune at the same time. My orientation was highly impractical and oriented toward the spirit realms. I hitchhiked around the country, slept in a tent in the woods, dedicated myself to arcane studies, writing, dreamwork, and yoga. Then I became the apprentice to a

Venezuelan astrologer. I was following a somewhat unusual path. There were many implications of these developments. I experienced notable tension in my relationships with family members, friends and former friends, who didn't feel that being a yogi-astrologer was a viable career path. Holding a steady job was problematic. I spent my early twenties feeling strange and often ridiculed for my interests in astrology, mysticism, and metaphysics. The Saturnian skepticism of our culture is such that some of us feel embarrassed about these noble pursuits. But at the time of this crucial transit I set in motion the direction of my adult life. I set my own course and I remained committed to it. At this time I also attempted to actualize my individuality through music. My natal Uranus and Venus are in close aspect, so this phase of my Uranus cycle included attempts to express myself musically. I was an earnest street-corner musician.

The other phases of the Uranus cycle are also significant moments to move forward in unfolding our individuality; the trine, sesquiquadrate, even the quincunx of Uranus to its natal position are all worth examining closely. But the most potent phase of the cycle is Uranus' opposition to its birth position at about 40–42 years of age. The Uranus opposition at midlife is a crucial turning point because at this time we can reappraise our lives and find ways to more fully actualize our idealistic, youthful life dreams—which may have been set aside to attend to the necessary Saturnian tasks of building our life structures. These unrealized potentials now demand attention and ask to be lived more fully. Intense urges for freedom, self-expression, change, and self-actualization arise within us. For those following an individuated path, evolution accelerates at the Uranus full moon phase. At my Uranus opposition I felt an irresistible urge to start playing music again after years of neglecting this side of myself. I did several performances in public and on the radio. I also participated in a remarkable musical training through the Berkeley Jazz Workshop. Musically, I went in new directions. Uranus inspires us to take whatever steps are necessary to live the wholeness of who we are.

As we individuate we may feel that we stand apart from the collective in some aspects of our lifestyle, beliefs, or commitments. This may mean bearing isolation from the herd. Uranus is the principle of mutation. When we mutate, others may view us as fools, and we may feel like outsiders, living on the edge of conventional society. But gradually we accept that one condition of our freedom is to bear the discomfort of following an unconventional path. Uranus frees us from bondage to convention. It is impersonal in attitude, seemingly impervious to criticism or doubt. The task simply must be done. It is the will of the universe, and we are the instruments for carrying out its intentions. What I find most interesting is finding that point of balance where we are stable and functional within Saturn's realm of convention and mainstream society, but where we are also responsive to Uranus so that we express our unique Uranian genius and talents in ways that influence our culture.[40]

The condition of the seed is a useful metaphor for the Uranian crisis of liberation, as Rudhyar often said. Do we live as decaying leaves, bound by the doctrines, values, and assumptions of a decaying industrial culture—which are increasingly shaped by the global news-entertainment- disinformation media, which encourages us to live primarily as consumers in a society saturated with advertising, numbing ourselves to global environmental breakdown? Or do we become seed persons, dedicated to a future cycle of existence? Uranus says: Assume the condition of a seed, "pregnant with a living futurity."[41] Become the root and origin of new life, of future cycles of cultural rebirth. You are of the new world, leave the old behind. All it takes is the courage to change.[42]

Uranus governs the process of invention that enables us to invent our own unusual social identities. For some people this means freedom from traditional kinds of employment. Uranus is a crucial planet for the growing numbers of people who have become self-employed, independent contractors. While the uncertainty of this lifestyle is sometimes nerve-wracking, Uranus teaches us to be grateful if we are able to set our own schedule, and live according to our own rhythms. Of course, Uranus is also about adaptation to rapid changes in collective patterns of living, including those due to the impact of new inventions and technologies. For some people this means exploring electronic culture and internet commerce, while others feel excitement about new developments in biotechnology, space travel, or digital audio recording technology. Uranus makes us aware that we need to adapt, get up to speed, and keep contemporary, or we will be left in the dust. Uranus also represents attunement to the forces of politics, social change and cultural revolution. Thus, attunement to Uranus implies doing our part to further the great Work of humanity's awakening and our planetary evolution toward a new consciousness.

Neptune

The next station of our journey to freedom is Neptune, lord of the fog, dissolver of certainties, revealer of expanded consciousness. Neptune symbolizes receptivity to the current of grace, which restores us to full union with our source, the great Ocean, the eternal light of consciousness. Neptune is a planet of highs and lows, agony and ecstasy. It symbolizes watery initiations that require surrender, trust, letting go. Things may fall apart or be at a complete standstill in our lives. Always a test of faith in the unknown is involved. In the end, if all goes well, we receive a blessing, the descent of peace.

Neptune represents a state of liquidity, an experience of being pulled by an invisible spiritual undertow beyond the shores of ordinary consciousness. We feel soft, liquid, fluid. In alchemy, this process is called *solutio*, the dissolution of the base metal (lead) of the ego so that it can be transformed into gold. We experience ourselves being melted down. Psychologically, we feel weak, uncertain, confused, helpless, indecisive, unsure of our direction, spacey, or dependent. In Jungian terms, we experience a descent to the unconscious, an upwelling of images, memories, and feelings from the deep unconscious. The Neptune *solutio* stage is often marked by dream symbols of baths, showers, sprinkling, swimming, immersion in water, baptism, or drowning.[43] These are symbols of immersion in the unconscious, and conscious relationship to the unconscious; they herald a restoration of our original wholeness. They also symbolize a dissolving of boundaries and solidified ego structures that restrict our vision of reality. I describe a dream with this type of watery symbolism in Chapter 4.

If Saturn is about maturity and mastery in the outer world, Neptune is about exploring inner space and subtle, transpersonal realms of consciousness. Neptune represents our natural evolutionary urge to experience Unity consciousness, awareness of our spiritual source and final destination. Neptune governs all experiences in which we transcend the ordinary boundaries of space and time, for example, experiences of precognition or images of past lives, or a sense of unity with other people or other life forms—with plants, animals, mountains, the earth itself. We feel the interconnectedness of everything. We may intuitively know the thoughts of others and experience that telepathy is real. When transiting Uranus squared my natal Neptune I traveled through South India with my father. One night we checked into a hotel room, turned on the light in the bathroom and found a cockroach the size of an armadillo. Being a good, nonviolent, spiritual kind of person, I picked up my Birkenstock sandal and thwacked the cockroach as hard as I could. The carcass was duly disposed of. The next day we were riding a bus for many hours. At one point we both dozed off and an hour or so passed without our speaking a word. Then I turned to my dad and said, "I could kick myself for not taking a photo of that cockroach. Nobody is going to believe us when we tell them how enormous it was." My father's face turned white and he looked stunned. He said to me, "I was just thinking the exact same thing." At the Neptune level we become open to synchronicity, the meaningful coincidence of events.

Neptune is a very psychic planet. One day when transiting Sun and Neptune were conjunct in the sky I was talking to an Indian shopkeeper (back home in California) and I told him I was an astrologer. He asked me, "What does it mean when you think something and then it happens? Yesterday I was thinking about someone I hadn't seen in three years, and this morning he walked into my store." I said it means that the two of you are connected, and that such experiences remind us that our perceptions of boundaries and distance between us are ultimately illusory.

During Neptune transits and progressions we may experience the healing power of dreams, and become interested in the mysteries of the dream state. Dreams play many roles in our lives. They help us to process feelings, digest recent experience, rehearse tasks and upcoming situations; and work through traumas and forgotten memories. Dreams aid in memory processing and problem-solving, make us aware of emerging medical conditions, give us insight into our relationships, and reveal our next steps.[44] Emotionally and spiritually, they can be deeply redemptive. Dreams also have much to teach us about the nature of consciousness. Out-of-body experience during dreams, telepathy and clairvoyance in dreams, lucid dreaming, dreams of mandalas or other psychedelic types of imagery, and white light experiences in dreams are all phenomena suggesting that the true nature of our consciousness is infinite and unbound. According to dream researcher Harry Hunt, human consciousness has an intrinsic tendency toward reflexivity or self-reference, and the psyche often represents itself in dreams involving mandalas or white light.[45] Images or experiences of white light in dreams reflect a turning inward of our awareness back to the most basic quality of visual-spatial perception, namely its *luminosity*. According to Hunt, luminosity or light is the cross-cultural metaphor for experiences of an absolute unity behind the diversity of appearance. Just as an artist paints a self-portrait, consciousness portrays its own activity in dreams with mandala or white light imagery, where the luminosity of awareness is translated into tactile-kinesthetic patterns. In this way, awareness becomes aware of its own nature.

While transiting Neptune was conjunct my Sun, I had this dream: I am in a meditation class. The teacher, a woman, gives me a quick karate chop to my back. Everything dissolves into nothingness and blissful, formless white light. During the Uranus-Neptune conjunction in 1993 I had another dream: I saw and felt, in a flash, the white light of pure consciousness. Neptune symbolizes our experience of the light of consciousness, whether in dreams, in meditation, or in the waking state.

When transiting Neptune turned stationary direct exactly square my natal Neptune, I stayed up late one night rereading Rudhyar's book, *Rhythm of Wholeness*. I read this passage:

> Between the symbolic Moon and Sunset of the cycle of being the fundamental goal of evolution is the consummation of the "divine Marriage" of spirit and matter within a human being. In this union of opposites, the all-encompassing meaning of Wholeness is revealed in a moment of Illumination, in a moment of dynamic equilibrium in which the principles of Unity and Multiplicity are of equal strength. The union must be contained within a form that can resist the union's intense "heat" and not be shattered by it. This form is the mind of wholeness—a mind totally filled with the harvest of a long series of life experiences that were spirit oriented yet rooted in the substance of earthly existence. When this mind reaches a perfected state of development, karma is fulfilled. . . . Man is potentially the complete manifestation of Wholeness. To be such a manifestation is man's *dharma*, and the field for such a manifestation has to be given form by the mind of wholeness—the mind illumined by spirit.[46]

In the morning I woke up with this dream: I was visiting a house. Somebody informed me that Rudhyar had just died, and his body was upstairs. Did I want to see him? I climbed a staircase and entered the room where his body was. Rudhyar was lying on a bed on his side, with both arms reaching over his head. His eyes were wide open, gazing into the radiant luminosity of the infinite. He was looking directly into the Light. This image lasted only for a moment, but it was incredibly vivid. I was jolted awake by that luminosity.

Like any dream, I interpret this on many levels. The dream portrays my inner image of Rudhyar's reflection on the eternal Light, his turning toward it throughout his life but with greater constancy and urgency in his final years. The "meaning" of the dream is also the *effect* it had on me, which was profound. The dream is what Mircea Eliade (another great philosopher) calls a *hierophany*, an eruption or manifestation of the sacred, the numinous.[47] Rudhyar's eyes are gazing into the luminosity of Being, but also *reveal* that luminosity. The dream felt like a transmission: Rudhyar is the agency or instrument that allows me to perceive the Light with my own eyes. The dream bestows on me the living experience of Rudhyar's Mind of Wholeness, spontaneously revealing itself in the moment of illumination. I feel that the dream was also my internal reverie on the evolution of a great being's consciousness. It can be interpreted as an intuitive perception of Rudhyar's ultimate liberation into the light of Consciousness, his movement in the after-death *bardo* realms toward the final freedom. His body passes on but the light shines radiantly through his work, his ideas, his life, who he was. The dream is also a teaching for me, revealing wisdom about death as a transition into the great Light. This dream renewed my internal relationship with one of my most significant teachers.

During Neptune transits or progressions we may develop greater fervor for enlightenment or union with the divine. We feel an urge to plunge deeper in meditation. Our longing for liberation intensifies. We perceive the one Spirit that underlies the world of multiplicity and material forms. All duality dissolves into serene, non-dual awareness. We transcend our false identification with the physical body, the mind, our emotions and desires, and awaken as the Self, the vast silence and divine light and power that dwell within us. We merge into the radiance of pure consciousness. We taste limitless Being, Love Absolute. A woman named Nina had transiting Neptune conjunct natal

Sun for two years, and transiting Pluto conjunct natal Neptune in the 11th house (Chart #15). She joined a spiritual community (11th house Neptune), where she spent days and weeks in deep, silent meditation, and experienced *samadhi*—that state where thought stops, the breath stops, and one merges into the ocean of Being.

At times the transition into an expanded awareness is quite confusing. Susan, a woman with a natal Sun-Neptune conjunction in Libra in the 4th house, was experiencing transiting Neptune conjunct her Descendant (Chart #16). She was in crisis, she said, because "my marriage is falling apart" (a very Neptunian experience). Susan also had solar arc Uranus conjunct natal Mars: She was intensely angry at her husband. A deeply spiritual woman who had practiced meditation for many years, she was learning now that anger is okay, and that she doesn't have to be selfless all the time. There is a place for the expression of her will. She began having intense *kundalini* experiences, feeling intense heat in her body (Uranus conjunct Mars) and the rising serpent energy flowing through her body in powerful spirals.

Susan was concerned because during this Neptune transit she had totally lost all sexual desire for her husband. Her awareness was turned inward and she experienced many movements of subtle internal energies and opening of *chakras* (subtle energy centers) in meditation. She wondered if she should leave her husband. With transiting Neptune conjunct her De-

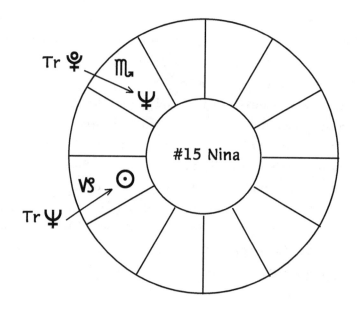

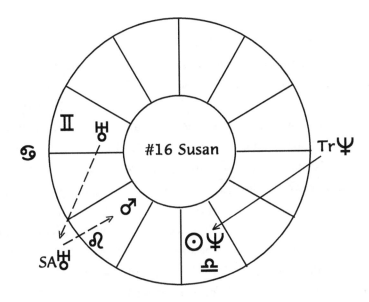

scendant and square her natal Sun in the 4th house in Libra, she realized that marriage and family are everything to her, so she could not leave her husband. Yet she could feel Neptune uplifting her vibrationally to a new level of consciousness. The tide of her being was flowing directly into the light of Spirit. Rudhyar calls Neptune a planet of *deconditioning*. Susan's attitudes toward marriage and love were being deconditioned. She could no longer be the embodiment of her husband's desires and expectations. She could no longer mold herself to his needs, for her need now was to dissolve and be etheric. She experienced some disillusionment (Neptune) with her very earthly, needy, human beloved. But slowly she began to meet him from a deeper place of unconditional acceptance. They had several powerful telepathic experiences during this period, and when they meditated together there was often a descent of peace and grace tangible to both of them. They experienced a shared awakening and were able to reconnect to the awareness of loving each other's essence beyond form and beyond desire. Their marriage continued and reached a new level of union and devotion.

Transits and progressions involving Neptune can be especially turbulent and disruptive if we are in the grip of addiction, denial, avoidance of reality, or in a state of unhealthy dependency. Chris, whose natal Sun in his 5th house opposed Neptune in the 11th house, told me that his spiritual practice was to take cocaine and speed and go out dancing all night in clubs, where he claimed to have ecstatic experiences (Chart #17). Chris needed to come to grips with his addictions and to find healthier expressions of his desire for ecstasy and expanded consciousness. A woman named Tracy with natal Neptune in the 4th house, square her natal Sun, comes from an extended family with rampant alcoholism. She herself has grappled with substance abuse. Tracy now attends 12 Step meetings and pursues a spiritual practice to uplift herself. James, a 46-year-old devout Christian who had always abstained from drugs and alcohol, attended a ceremony in which he ingested the Amazonian psychedelic *ayahuasca* while transiting Uranus squared his natal Neptune and solar arc Neptune was conjunct his Sun. James had a profound religious experience that confirmed and deepened his faith. He felt no strong desire to repeat the experience of ingesting *ayahuasca*, but he said he could now appreciate the place and value of entheogens when approached reverently, in a sacred manner, as an aid and ally along the spiritual path.[48]

Neptune may temporarily weaken our will and sense of self-determination. We may grapple with discouragement or loss of focus. Yet this is our moment of greatest potential access to the Sacred, the living Spirit. We may feel that we do not know what is happening to us and that it is completely out of our hands what happens. We need to strive to cope with the material world and with our emotions, so that we are not in denial. Yet if we are fulfilling our

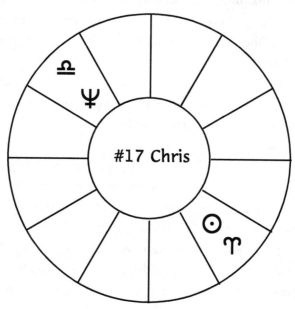

responsibilities to the best of our abilities, it is fully appropriate to cultivate faith, tranquility, and contentment during Neptune's visitations, trusting that everything is unfolding as it should. This offering of our trust to the universe brings peace to our hearts, and is one of Neptune's greatest gifts.

A strong Saturn can be an important steadying influence as we navigate Neptune's formless territories. Neptune symbolizes the awareness that there are no limits. This awareness coexists with our Saturnian awareness of the reality of limits. The periodic transiting aspects between Saturn and Neptune (every 8.5 years; their actual cycle is 35 years) represent a continuous dance between our dreams and ideals, and the practical realities of the world. At times this can feel very discouraging and disappointing, as if our worldly lives and responsibilities bind our spirits and the reality of our current circumstances falls short of our ideal. Yet astrology instructs us in each step of the slow process of building our dreams (Saturn-Neptune). Through the continuing tests and pressures of Saturn we overcome Neptune's weakness and arouse confidence in our ability to concretize our inner visions. Mastering the conditions of this world, this culture, this social environment, we also receive the deepest inpouring of grace and spiritual blessings. We become grounded vessels (Saturn) into which Spirit flows (Neptune), where its radiance and love can be embodied and expressed in well-crafted forms—in our careers, in our relationships and emotional attachments with others, in our life structures. Limitless possibilities are unfolding on planet earth, and we are the instrument, as we manifest, one step at a time, our dreams, our visions, to incarnate our archetypal and spiritual potentials. The goal of astrological self-study is to become an *avatar* of oneself, to bring about what Rudhyar calls, "the union of the precisely differentiated divine and the perfectly integrated human—an avatar or divine manifestation. This is the marriage of heaven and earth."[49] Holding the balance of Saturn and Neptune, we master our resistance to material incarnation, our fear of failure, our sense of disappointment, and patiently build the edifice of our freedom. Our birthmaps provide a detailed map of the ways we are each to incarnate the "precisely differentiated divine."

A crucial gift of Neptune is compassionate response to the suffering that is everywhere around us, which connects us to the experience of all humanity. Neptune washes our hardened hearts with the wine of concern, and awakens in us the intention to relieve suffering. Neptune transits are opportunities to transmute our personal suffering, and to awaken the compassion of a *bodhisattva*, responsive to the sorrow and suffering of all beings.

A major Neptune problem is self-pity, the tendency to feel sorry for ourselves. We feel like Job struggling with Yahweh, bewailing our fate, wondering, Why me? Neptune periods may be characterized by what Edward Edinger calls *ego-Self alienation*, in which, losing contact with the Self, the transpersonal ground and source of the ego, we experience depression, despair, emptiness, and feelings of guilt, sin, or unworthiness.[50] In religious language, the individual feels estranged from God, the creator. The king is wounded or sick, the kingdom is barren, and it seems that nothing can make things right. But the depression of the wounded king, symbol of the ego's defeat and alienation from its source, is but the precursor to the moment when the light reveals itself to us, as the *numinosum*, the sacred, as autonomous Power. Edinger calls this *restoration of the ego-Self axis*, the rediscovery of the relationship between the ego and its spiritual and archetypal ground. Edinger writes,

> The classic symbol for alienation is the image of the wilderness. And it is here, characteristically, that some manifestation of God is encountered. When the wanderer lost in the desert is about to perish, a source of divine nourishment appears. The Israelites in the wilderness are fed by *manna* from heaven. Elijah in the wilderness is fed by ravens. . . Psychologically this means that the experience of the supporting aspect of the archetypal psyche is most likely to occur when the ego has exhausted its own resources and is aware of its essential impotence by itself . . . At a certain point . . , usually after an intense alienation experience, the ego-Self axis suddenly breaks into conscious view. . . The ego becomes aware, experientially, of a transpersonal center to which the ego is subordinate . . . Whenever man consciously encounters a divine agency which assists, commands or directs, we can understand it as an encounter of the ego with the Self.[51]

Neptune symbolizes this discovery of a transpersonal center and a divine agency that commands and directs us. The redemptive drama of a lengthy Neptune transit or progression may bring us to an absolute low point where we are greatly humbled and thus ready to receive an infusion of spiritual light. Now we feel the intervention of a guiding intelligence that actively seeks to illuminate our paths and to make us whole. Some call this the *guru*, or the spirit of guidance. Jung called this the Self, the archetype of wholeness. There is something inside us that actively assists in unfolding the wholeness of what we are in our essence, in our archetypal and spiritual core (which is what the birth chart as a whole depicts). Von Franz writes,

> The individuation process is more than a coming to terms between the in-born germ of wholeness and the outer acts of fate. Its subjective experience conveys the feeling that some supra-personal force is actively intervening in a creative way. One sometimes feels that the unconscious is leading the way in accordance with a secret design. It is as if something is looking at me, something that I do not see but that sees me. . . . The ego must be able to listen attentively and to give itself, without any further design or purpose, to that inner urge toward growth. . . . [I]n order to bring the individuation process into reality, one must surrender consciously to the power of the unconscious. . . One must simply listen, in order to learn what the inner totality—the Self—wants one to do here and now in a particular situation.[52]

One of the ways we discern the intention of the Self is through dreams. I have had hundreds of dreams that have revealed to me the wisdom and guidance of the unconscious. Here is one of them. I had this dream when transiting Neptune was conjunct my Moon and during the turbulence of the Uranus opposition—a crucial period when I was grappling with a two-fold failure. I had published my fourth book, *The Nine Stages of Spiritual Apprenticeship*, which I consider by far my best book, a book that I was sure was going to do very well. Unfortunately the book didn't sell well at all, and I lost a lot of money. Also, I was encountering obstacles in my search for a teaching job that I hoped would provide me with a secure income. I was experiencing a profound defeat of the ego on a number of fronts.[53] It was in this context that I had this dream: A young man (a symbol of the *puer eternus*, the archetype of youth) is waving his arms at airplanes that are hovering overhead (note the Neptunian theme of being "up in the air"). Suddenly the young man falls to the ground stricken by a heart attack. A woman tries to resuscitate him, but the man is fading fast. I walk over to where he is lying on the ground. I bring my palms together in the *namasté* gesture and then hold my hands out in a gesture of surrender, acceptance, and letting go. He sees this, and at that moment the man dies.

The young man waving his hands in a futile gesture symbolizes my personal struggle for success in these ventures. It is my own state of ego-Self alienation and feelings of anguish and futility. It is unclear in the dream whether the planes hovering overhead are waiting to land, or if they are waiting to take off. This suggests my questions and doubts about whether I would ever land, get grounded in my life, and if my work would ever "take off." The man's death is a symbol of the death of this struggle. I needed to recognize that I had done everything I could to market my book and to find a teaching job, but now it was out of my hands; all that struggle needed to die. The puer's grandiose dreams of success as a writer and teacher had to die. Dream images tend to exaggerate in order to portray our inner condition, and to cast our situation in an archetypal light. Here the psyche's symbol-forming function accurately portrayed my feeling that I was dying inside; also, my discouragement—literally a loss of heart, a "heart attack." I have never before had such a clear image and *experience* of the death of the ego.

Responding to the final image of the dream, I tried to let go and accept things the way they are. I immersed myself in the spiritual practices of yoga, dreamwork, meditation, astrology, and music. I felt very soft, very humble. I found peace through acceptance of God's Will. I tried to cultivate contentment with a simple life. And when I bottomed out and surrendered myself a miraculous thing happened: I was lifted up by a higher power. Fortune called. After *seven years* of searching for a university teaching position I was hired at John F. Kennedy University's Graduate School for Holistic Studies, where I now teach courses exploring human development and life cycles, Jungian psychology, transpersonal counseling, yoga, dreamwork, and the philosophy of holism. I throw in a little astrology too, when appropriate. This job is far better than any situation I could have imagined. It was only when I had given up completely and offered myself in service that the miraculous occurred. Grace descended. And the book still didn't sell much. There are some things in life that just don't work out. It is not the divine will.

To the extent that we cling to our certainties, we resist the formless ambiguity of Neptune. Neptune is always *a test of faith*, faith in the hidden order and secret design of life, which can at times take us right to the precipice of uncertainty. It is such a blessing to be able to understand such experiences in the light of astrology. In *Therapeutic Astrology*, I discussed astrology as a container for chaotic, transitional periods. We might feel very confused during a Neptune transit but knowing the planetary symbolism can reassure us as we pass through this disorienting meltdown. We learn the wisdom of *not knowing,* and the trust that all will be revealed to us. We need to practice meditation and prayer and try to keep the faith, surrendering as deeply as we can. Then the moment of profound personal redemption comes when we feel blessed by something greater than ourselves.

Neptune transits are lessons in surrender, equanimity, and receptivity. We encounter a power and intention that is greater than our conscious will. It is more far-seeing and infinitely wiser. We do well to turn to it often for guidance and illumination of our purpose. Neptune represents the salvational quality of the divine. We are touched by grace, and filled with peace and gratitude knowing that our lives are blessed and guided.

Rudhyar taught that the key that opens the door to a transpersonal consciousness is *self-consecration,* offering ourselves to a greater whole. We offer our lives as instruments of healing and transformation, in whatever form it may take. When I was 25 years old and had transiting Saturn conjunct natal Neptune I consciously experienced a distinct moment of self-consecration. I was walking the streets of Madison, Wisconsin looking for a job, when I stopped on the sidewalk and cried out inwardly, "Let me do something that will be of service in this world. Let my efforts be of benefit to others and contribute to the healing of the planet." At that moment I felt a blissful descent of peace. My body trembled as I received the rain of grace. My prayer had been heard. When we inwardly offer ourselves there is an immediate response from the cosmos, the greater Whole, and we are guided to the next steps we need to take to fulfill the purpose of our birth.

To understand the deepest implications of Neptune as a symbol of our growing self-surrender and alignment with a higher evolutionary power, contemplate these words from Sri Aurobindo's masterwork, *The Synthesis of Yoga:*

> The process of Yoga is a turning of the human soul from the egoistic state of consciousness absorbed in the outward appearances and attraction of things to a higher state in which the Transcendent and Universal can pour itself into the individual mould and transform it. . . . But in proportion as this contact establishes itself, the Sadhaka [spiritual aspirant] must become conscious that a force other than his [her] own, a force transcending his [her] egoistic endeavor and capacity, is at work in him [her] and to this Power s/

he learns progressively to submit himself and delivers up to it the charge of his [her]Yoga. In the end his [her] own will and force become one with the higher Power; s/he merges them in the divine Will and its transcendent and universal Force. S/He finds it thenceforward presiding over the necessary transformation of his [her] mental, vital, and physical being with an impartial wisdom and provident effectivity of which the . . . ego is not capable. . . . Purified, liberated, plastic, illumined, it can begin to serve as a means for the direct action of a supreme Power in the larger Yoga of humanity or superhumanity, of the earth's spiritual progression or its transformation. When the human ego . . . learns to trust itself to that which transcends it, that is its salvation.

The inner Guide, the World-Teacher. . . destroys our darkness by the resplendent light of his knowledge; that light becomes within us the increasing glory of his own self-revelation. He discloses progressively in us his own nature of freedom, bliss, love, power, and immortal being. He sets above us his divine example as our ideal and transforms the lower existence into a reflection of that which it contemplates. . . . The full recognition of this inner Guide, Master of the Yoga, lord, light, enjoyer, and goal of all sacrifice and effort, is of the utmost importance in the path of integral perfection. This inner Guide is often veiled at first by the very intensity of our personal effort and by the ego's preoccupation with itself and its aims. As we gain in clarity and the turmoil of egoistic effort gives place to a calmer self-knowledge, we recognize the source of the growing light within us. . . . . We feel the presence of a supreme Master, Friend, Lover, Teacher. We recognize it in the essence of our being as that develops into likeness and oneness with a greater and wider existence; for we perceive that this miraculous development is not the result of our own efforts; an eternal Perfection is moulding us into its own image. . . . The surest way toward this integral fulfillment is to find the Master of the secret who dwells within us, open ourselves constantly to the divine Power which is also the divine Wisdom and Love and trust to it to effect the conversion.

My way. . . is to go inward into oneself, to open by aspiration to the Divine and once one is conscious of it and its action, to give oneself to it entirely. This self-giving means not to ask for anything but the constant contact or union with the Divine Consciousness, to aspire for its peace, power, light and felicity [happiness], but to ask nothing else and in life and action to be its instrument only for whatever work it gives one to do in the world. If one can once open and feel the Divine Force, the Power of the Spirit working in the mind and heart and body, the rest is a matter of remaining faithful to it, calling for it always, allowing it to do its work when it comes and rejecting every other and inferior force that belongs to the lower consciousness and the lower nature.[54]

Neptune transits and progressions are times to deepen our self-offering to the divine and to become aware of the mysterious inner Guide, which gradually reveals its plans for us, and opens doors in our lives that are compatible with our true and highest purpose.

Most of us start out using astrology to fulfill our personal desires, and it can be very helpful toward that end. Indeed, if we consciously cooperate with the cycles of life we tend to be more successful in our endeavors. (See "Strategically Timed Action" in Chapter 4.) But over time we also experience the freedom of transcending our desires as we cooperate with the universal will, with the Master of the Great Work. We begin to grasp that, at any given moment, a life-path is open to us that emphasizes certain archetypal themes and possibilities, and not others. We sense how this path asks us to fulfill certain conditions and responsibilities for our benefit and growth, and ulti-mately for the betterment of the Whole. We are at peace as we surrender to the unfolding order, the natural way of things, in alignment with planetary rhythms.

As we study our charts it is helpful to ask not just, What do I want?, but also, What is my responsibility to the universe? What does life want me to do now? Is it to make money, to make music, to make a child, to grow food, to meditate, to write a book, to go to school, to create community with others? We embrace the path that is revealed to us as our right road. We sense who and what life wants us to become. *We cooperate with whatever wants to unfold, to the best of our ability to discern this through astrological study.* Indeed, this is the essence of the whole matter. We view the planetary symbolism of our birth charts and transits as a roadmap and a directive, guiding our actions and choices.

Approached reverently as an agency of instruction by the Guide, the inner Teacher, astrology begins to train us and prepare us for who we are supposed to become. We strive to mold our intention to the intention of the universe, even if at first it doesn't conform to what we think we want. Once I had a very intense experience doing a fifteen-minute chart reading for someone at a fair: Laura had transiting Saturn conjunct natal Venus in Aries, opposite natal Neptune. She was in love with a married man who lives across the country. It was a classic love tragedy. He promised to divorce his wife, someday, so he and Laura could be together. But for the moment she was left alone, waiting, longing, with everything up in the air (Neptunian ambiguity). She was quite sad. I asked Laura to consider that perhaps a hidden purpose of this situation was to connect her to an experience of love transcending place and time. I asked her to open to a love transcending needs or expectations, a pure love for all beings. That love was already shining brightly from her heart; and the connection she felt with this man reminded her that love is her true nature. This was her path to awakening, to embody unconditional love (Venus-Neptune). I asked her to meditate on how her own suffering could awaken in her boundless compassion for all beings. I asked her to let the small vessel of personal love and attachment burst so that she could expand her heart to encompass all. When I said these words Laura began to breathe deeply through her heart. She lit up and her eyes brightened. We sat together for a while quietly, looking around at all the people at the fair with unconditional love. She began to laugh and said, "I'm feeling strangely ecstatic, which I find hard to understand since I feel like I'm supposed to be feeling miserable and torn up about this relationship." The words I spoke came forth from me quite spontaneously as I meditated upon her chart symbolism. I had never met her or seen her chart before. I could have just as easily focused on the tragedy of unrequited love or gently chided her for her romantic illusions. Instead, I tried to evoke the highest possible meaning of the transit and of her natal Venus-Neptune. I tried to help her perceive a hidden cause or intention of these events. Everything happens for a reason. This interpretation of her chart allowed Laura to expand her perception of her situation so that she might fulfill the purpose of this transit. In *The Astrology of Transformation*, Dane Rudhyar wrote:

> In transpersonal living, an individual should not be concerned with "success" and especially with what from the socio-cultural point of view would be called a constructive achievement. . . . An individual on the transpersonal path should realize in what way a present occurrence is an *effect* of the past, and . . . understand the *purpose* of the event in generating power to move ahead in the process of transformation. . . . [T]he real issue is whether [one remains] as unaware as before of the *inherent transformative purpose* of the events, or whether the individual will be able to meet these happenings as tools for the cutting and grinding of the coarse and dull stone of personality into a clear and translucent jewel.[55]

Nowhere else could Laura find this type of understanding except through astrology. All her friends could perceive, and all she herself had perceived until now, was a failure, a love affair that didn't work out. Now she could see that through this painful experience, her heart was being transformed. On an emotional level she still felt sadness. Yet she felt much more connected to everyone and began to perceive beauty everywhere. As Hazrat Inayat Khan once said, "Out of the shell of the broken heart emerges the newborn soul."[56]

Laura learned the Neptunian lesson that sometimes we have to yield our desires. She recognized that this was a time to awaken universal love and inner communion with the light in everyone. Her deeper essence knew that life was asking her to be absorbed in a state of consciousness that transcends longing and loneliness. Several weeks later she called to tell me that after the fair she was actively cultivating, and radiating, this divine love and perceiving the light of Spirit everywhere, in everything. We were both thankful for the way the planetary symbolism of Venus-Neptune had evoked for us insight into the transformative potential of her predicament. This is the power of astrology, the power to transform how we view our circumstances and our suffering.[57]

Neptune transits enable us to lift our consciousness beyond mundane concerns, beyond the anxious struggle for survival, to turn within in union with the Source. We continue to resolve issues at the socio-cultural and individual levels. Remember that Saturn's tasks are unending; we grow in knowledge of who we are as individuals and how we can contribute to society. But under Neptune's influence we also feel a tidal pull toward meditation, and to merge directly into the Absolute. Here planetary symbols can lead us to the gate, but we must walk through it ourselves, directly, experientially, through meditation.

Recently I have had an interesting change in my own meditation practice. After years of meditating alone in a room with my legs crossed in lotus position, now I like to go outside in nature and practice meditation standing up, preferably near a tree, with my hands in one of two gestures or *mudras*. A mudra is a gesture, a reminder that puts us in another state of consciousness. I'd like to teach these mudras to you now. First, place your hands out with your palms facing up, in a gesture of receptivity, feeling like an empty vessel, ready to receive guidance and assistance, open, surrendered, serene. This is the practice of alignment of the personal will with the universal will.

"I want whatever is best for the greater Whole." As you do this, think of a current transit or progression, and ask for insight and illumination.

The second gesture is to raise your arms up with your index fingers pointing outward, into space. As you do this, radiate light from your heart, sending forth your clearest emanation, and project mental images of your unfolding road and its desired qualities, invoking the future and literally drawing it toward yourself. Invoke images of the optimal potential outcome of this planetary symbol. Once you get the idea of projecting the image forward in your mind's eye you can bring your arms down. I call this principle the formative use of will, the *kriya shakti,*[58] the power of visualization as a form of *invocatory magic*—an essential skill for any initiate on the Path. Indeed, *I now define astrology as the use of the formative will guided by planetary symbolism for the purpose of unfolding our evolutionary potential.*

The higher evolutionary astrology is practiced by emanating from our higher centers, from the levels of Neptune and Pluto. Here we harness the combined power of Imagination and Will. Neptune and Pluto together represent the power of grace to transform our lives; the power of the Whole to disclose itself, and to make the power of the Whole available to us, as we merge our consciousness and will with the divine consciousness and the divine will. Neptune-Pluto as a planetary pair comprise the guru function: revealer of the light, the grace-bestowing power of God. More specifically, Pluto is the testing function, which asks us, as Aurobindo says, to reject "every inferior force belonging to the lower consciousness and the lower nature."[59]

Pluto

The Neptune experience of dissolution cannot be our final resting place, for life is unceasing cycles of evolution; there is no final end point. The stillness of *samadhi* or deep meditation is just one moment on the wheel of time. As the cycle of being continues, we eventually return to the moment where individual form emerges from the ocean of being, with the evolutionary task to *individualize,* to become a unique embodiment of eternal, archetypal spiritual qualities represented by the symbols of our birth charts. To prepare us to use our faculties and to fulfill our destiny as individuals in a way that is in alignment with the cosmic order and collective needs, we are put through the tests of Pluto, which remold our character and expose our imperfections.

Pluto prepares us to become agents of the universal Spirit, able to wield our powers, talents, and capacities effectively, yet with a purity of intention that has been cleansed of malice, selfishness, and injurious power drives. Pluto's initiations teach us to act as instruments for a purpose that transcends our own will and desire. Pluto transforms us from persons dominated by the three poisons of lust, greed, and hatred, into Bodhisattvas, transpersonal individuals, self-consecrated agents of the divine intention. For this to occur, the impurities of our personalities must be uprooted, through encountering the shadow side of our human nature—the mean-spiritedness, cruelty, hostility, resentment, and violence that lurk somewhere deep inside all of us.

If Saturn represents tests of responsibility, Uranus represents tests of individuation, and Neptune symbolizes tests of faith, then Pluto signifies tests of intention that teach us right use of will. Pluto transits and progressions refine our character and purify us of obsessions, fixations, and cravings, so the full power of life can flow through us unobstructed. Pluto aids us in the removal of impurities, brings matters to completion, and causes us to exhaust our karma on all levels.

A client of mine named Wendy had been living in a yoga ashram, practicing meditation and celibacy for several years (Chart #18). When transiting Pluto was conjunct her Descendant, she left the ashram and found herself magnetically attracted to Jack, an alcoholic plumber (very Plutonian) who hung around in pubs with criminals, bikers, speed freaks, and tough guys. She felt herself drawn to explore the parts of herself that this man and this environment evoked. She started smoking cigarettes and drinking heavily, adopting a cynical outlook quite in contrast to the outlook of the blissful, pure yogini. Jack was fiercely jealous and, on occasion, physically rough and intimidating. Yet Wendy liked this man and found him attractive while all the men in the ashram were, in her words, "emasculated wimps." Her rational mind fought all this, knowing Jack was wrong for her, that she wanted to walk on a spiritual path. She asked me what was happening to her, was she going crazy. It seemed that her evolution required her to visit the underworld, to complete her attraction to this life, as well as to exhaust definite karmic ties she had with Jack. At the third pass of Pluto over her Descendant, Wendy realized that she could no longer drink hard liquor; it

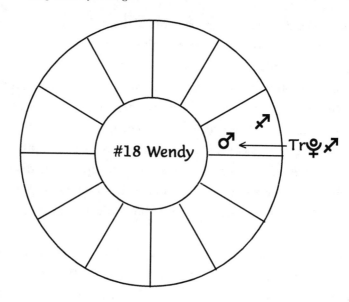

made her violently ill. She felt intense pressure in her head, as if a higher force was intervening and actively purifying her. She realized that she was vibrationally incompatible with Jack. During this one year transit of Pluto, Wendy completed her unfinished business with alcohol, cigarettes, and violence, and eventually stopped seeing him.

A fifty-year-old divorcee named Liz had transiting Saturn stationary retrograde square natal Pluto in her 11th house. When her 20-year-old niece came to stay with her for an extended visit she discovered that the young woman was dishonest, manipulative, hostile, and a bad influence on Liz's children. As Liz told me, "I finally said no more, I don't have to take care of her anymore, and I shipped her back home. Let her own mother deal with the hooligan!" Liz also distanced herself from a neighbor who had been spreading rumors about Liz to mutual friends (Pluto in 11th house: the circle of friends). This intolerable situation reminded her of how her role growing up in her family had been to take care of toxic people. She felt it was essential now to eliminate all the toxic people from her life, and so she did. But we cannot always hold the negative forces completely at bay.

Sometimes during transits or progressions involving Pluto, we encounter the negativity, cruelty, hatred, and destructiveness that exists in human nature. An African-American man named Leonard (Chart #19) encountered racism while traveling in the state of Texas, while transiting Saturn was conjunct natal Pluto in his 9th house and his progressed Moon was also

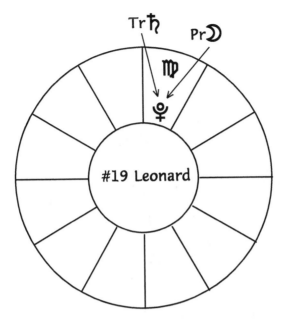

conjunct Pluto. This experience at age 20 made a deep impact on him and he went on to become a prominent attorney who fights for justice and human rights.

A woman from Iran named Fran was the target of several acts of racial hatred in her workplace while transiting Pluto was conjunct her natal Moon in the 6th house. She tried to understand, why? The question that arises at such moments, is whether we are so damaged and traumatized that we ourselves become armored, filled with hatred and resentment. Pluto governs elimination of all poisons from our nature, including toxic emotions; but first we experience them, encountering them in self and others. Pluto's initiations ask us to know the darkness that potentially lurks in all of us, the shadow. At certain times we must each meet and transform these forces in our lives.

Under Pluto's influence, we may need to release (volcanically at times) the accumulated pressure of unexpressed feelings, and to recover repressed insights or memories. A client named Anna, (Chart #20) with transiting Pluto conjunct her natal Sun-Saturn conjunction in the fourth house, had stunning realizations about the incestuous childhood relationship she had with her uncle; and she came to the decision to finally tell her parents, after a lifetime of depression and hiding the truth. The revelation of these secrets

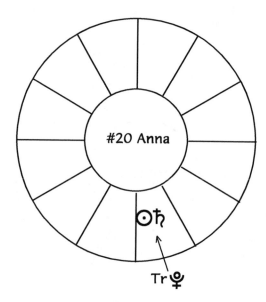

fell like a bomb on her family. Her father immediately cut off all contact with his brother, her uncle, causing a radical shift in the dynamics of the family. With Sun-Saturn in her 4th house, lots of responsibility had been placed on Anna since childhood. Now she realized that she didn't have to hide the truth to protect her parents; she is not responsible for their wellbeing. The tension caused by years of suppressed truth finally was released, causing profound family upheaval and an irrevocable rift between her father and uncle. These Plutonian events marked a moment of finality that cleared the way for new beginnings. There was no turning back.

Pluto often manifests in the form of disturbing events that hit us with the force of dynamite. An earthquake in Mexico or Guatemala or Iran. The hurricane storm that leaves a wake of destruction. The sudden death of a relative or a beloved public figure. A murder spree where innocents are gunned down at random. The Unabomber or the Oklahoma City bombing. The victims of concentration camps or forced labor gulags. Betrayal by a colleague or loved one. The destruction of forests. Watching a friend suffer from cancer or AIDS or chronic fatigue. Being the victim of a robbery or mugging, or the target of racism or sexism. Child abuse. Spousal abuse. Violence against animals. All of these realities evoke outrage, disbelief that life can be so cruel. Every day we are faced with Plutonian events and facts that shock us, shake us, make us feel sick at the violence in our midst. We reach out to meet the world with innocence and good intentions, yet we face so many things in this world that brutalize us and violate our right to live in safety and in peace.

Pluto sometimes symbolizes tests of pain that shatter our Neptunian innocence and idealism. Things are not as we think they ought to be. Pluto's function is to widen the sphere of awareness, sometimes through shock therapy, a rude awakening. Pluto teaches us that sometimes our paths include encounters with what is most destructive of the beauty of life. Pluto makes the underworld visible to us; it feels like a visitation of the darkness. We are left to ask, Why did this happen? How can people be so destructive? Under the influence of Pluto we may encounter someone who is filled with negativity or hatred. Or our own cruelty, malice, and destructiveness may be exposed. Only then can we begin to change. Only when we have seen the face of darkness can we become fully committed to the light. Only then do we begin to understand the need for refinement of our character. Pluto is the agent, and the symbol, of that purification and refinement of our personalities. Pluto's crises reorient our hearts, teaching us to consecrate our faculties and resources to the service of life.

If Pluto represents the pain of loss, grief, or bereavement, it also represents the healing we gain by letting go, releasing the bitterness, anger, and cynicism that we carry. Sometimes these feelings need expression. Sometimes we need to invoke Neptune, widening our hearts to enfold with our compassion both those who have been hurt by senseless violence but also those who, lost in ignorance, perpetrate it against others. Karen has Mars-Pluto in her 3rd house; when transiting Uranus opposed these planets a man moved into the apartment upstairs who is incredibly unfriendly, angry, and verbally abusive, a surly biker with an attitude. It would be easy for her to dislike him intensely. But Karen is a conscious person who practices meditation and studies astrology. She tries to relate to this man with compassion. She sees how he appeared in her life during a transit to *her* chart, *her* Mars-Pluto, so in some sense he represents a part of herself. Meher Baba once said that if you want to learn to love, start by loving those whom you think you cannot love. Whether we feel the force of dictatorial power wielded by a boss or government agency, or suffer cruel Plutonian punishment by the seeming whims of fate, we need to face evil without *becoming* it. Our goal should be

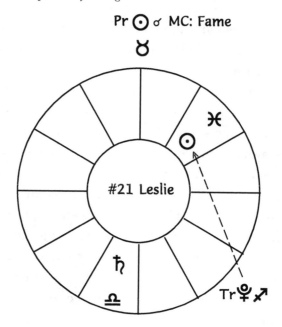

Pr ⊙ ♂ MC: Fame

to walk through the snake pits of life without becoming a snake ourselves. We confront the negativity of the collective shadow, without succumbing to it.

Leslie (Chart #21) was a successful businesswoman, and when her progressed Sun conjoined her MC she became something of a celebrity. But a few years later, transiting Pluto squared her natal Pisces Sun in the 8th house. She was accused of unethical business practices, was investigated by the government, and enveloped in scandal as the media created a web of lies about her. Reporters made unfounded claims, unjustly smearing her reputation. Simultaneously, her brother tried to take control of her business, an unexpected betrayal, a common manifestation of Pluto. (She has natal Saturn in the 3rd house of brothers). Leslie was eventually exonerated on all charges, but the business went bankrupt, details of her life were exposed by the media, and she felt completely naked and vulnerable. After this debacle, she sold everything and moved with her husband to a distant place with only two suitcases. She burned the fields behind her. She fought to defend her innocence, then she walked away. Somehow she came through this crisis with love toward her brother and all the reporters who had trashed her reputation. She said, "I feel completely clean in my actions. My conscience is clear. And I feel compassion for the people who tried to destroy me." This is

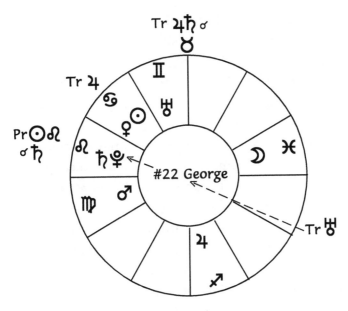

a positive evolutionary response to a Plutonian crisis. In the midst of losing everything and letting go of her past, Leslie came to embody more fully the compassion of her Pisces Sun.

At times, Pluto asks that we face death consciously. I recently met a man named George, who has AIDS and cancer (Chart #22). Natal Mars is in Virgo in his 1st house, and he has suffered from anxiety and chronic illness for most of his life (Mars rising in Virgo). With Sun-Venus conjunct in Cancer in the 11th house, he is a cook and gardener and has always sought community and to create a place of beauty where he and his friends could gather, celebrate, and heal. George has natal Saturn and Pluto conjunct in the 12th house; he has done much hospice work, and much inner work to overcome the fear of dying. George is committed to a spiritual practice involving helping others die, and consciously witnessing his own dying. With transiting Uranus in his 6th house opposite Saturn-Pluto, he has made heroic efforts to heal himself by every available alternative and natural health method. During Uranus opposite Saturn-Pluto he finally, at the age of 53, healed his relationship with his father (who had been abusive and cruel to George in childhood: Saturn-Pluto), winning his father's respect by the way he helped his mother die. With transiting Jupiter in Cancer conjunct his natal Sun-Venus, George is spending the summer at a rural alternative community where Jupiter has fulfilled his desire for spiritual community.

He is developing close emotional ties with several children in the community (11th house governs other people's children). He is teaching them lessons about cooking, gardening, and life that they will carry into the future. He hopes they remember him when he dies, which intuitively he knows will happen soon. Transiting Pluto is square his natal Ascendant: Each breath, each moment is precious to him now.

Pluto is the principle of endings and new beginnings. For example, transits of Pluto conjunct the Ascendant is often a time of radical personal change when we let go of aspects of our former lives. Here are four examples: a) A man with Libra rising who had been living the life of an ascetic yogi became very ill in India and nearly died. After this crisis his priorities changed and he became more interested in music, love, and relationships. b) A woman who had remained business partners with her ex-husband after their divorce severed all financial ties with him when Pluto was conjunct her Ascendant; her natal Pluto was in the 8th house of business partnership and joint finances. c) A man with Sagittarius rising resigned from his prestigious job in the field of publishing during a power struggle within his company. He went through a crisis as he let go of his cherished job title; then he found a new job that afforded him opportunities for learning and extensive travel. d) A metaphysical teacher and counselor with Sagittarius rising (and natal Sun conjunct Jupiter) had been in a reclusive period of misanthropy and despair. When Pluto passed over her Ascendant she re-emerged as a powerful, influential mind, expressing her knowledge through teaching and publishing her writings.

Pluto symbolizes the activity of the transpersonal will operative through the conscious individual who has consecrated every faculty—mind, heart, and will—to serve the Great Spirit, the principle of wholeness and healing. Pluto also symbolizes our capacity to develop some *shakti* in what we are doing, some power and effectiveness. We begin to emanate power and magnetism and to exert positive influence in our field of life.

A government lawyer named Dorothy with transiting Pluto conjunct her Sun/ IC in Sagittarius (zodiacal sign of the law) concluded a lengthy court case prosecuting a major corporation guilty of violating environmental laws (Chart #23). The corporation had spent tens of millions of dollars paying their own shark lawyers to fight the lawsuit at all costs. It seemed hopeless, but Dorothy fought on. She was totally exhausted, having given her all to the

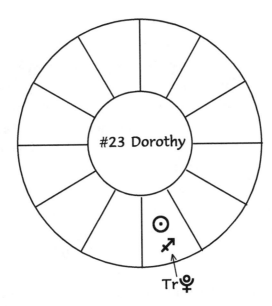

fight. The government won the case, and she felt she had triumphed for a moment over the forces of evil. She became the embodiment of (and conduit for) the archetype of Justice. Later, Dorothy resigned her position and was soon approached about running for public office.

Pluto teaches right use of will. When the power of the universe is behind us and we don't create obstructions with ego problems—such as arrogance, misuse of power, pride, grandiosity, greed, desire to dominate—then the power of the universe can flow through us, unimpeded. This is what occurs for us through attunement to Pluto, the planet symbolizing the capacity of the divine to reveal itself as limitless light, power, and unity of Being. We become supremely unified and one-pointed, focused like a laser beam in our intention. We merge our consciousness with the creative principle of the universe. We are fully in union in every faculty, in every dimension of our lives. We become adepts, masters of life, doers of great actions, a creative force in life's evolution. This is exactly what can happen for each of us if we prepare ourselves, if we meet each test of life skillfully. The universe needs us; humanity and the Earth need us. Each of us came here with an assignment, a work to unfold during this important moment of evolution.

Pluto makes us aware of the vortex of the apocalyptic forces that gather like thunderheads on our planet. We are faced with something much greater than our personal problems, namely our planetary destiny, including ultimate questions about our continued survival and how our lives are going to be affected by global climate changes. Plutonian events are often disturbing, shattering our dreams of how life is supposed to be—including vicious Middle East battles and Balkan wars, bombings and nuclear tests, terrorist acts of violence and destruction, abuses of human rights, toxicity and degradation of the environment, extinction of species and indigenous cultures, erupting volcanoes, earthquakes, global epidemics, El Nino, and strange weather patterns. Global warming has become a tangible reality. These "earth changes" are a balancing of our own karma, our own actions. They are Terra's response to our encroachment. There are simply too many of us producing too many waste products. Meanwhile, mighty corporate and political forces are pursuing their agendas of globalization, control, and accumulation of enormous wealth and power.

The myth of the Great Purification from Native American prophecy is a helpful guiding image to remember at this time. According to this myth, we are now living in the conditions of a great planetary cleansing. Some call it Tribulation, a time of karmic balancing, retribution, and purification for all beings. Many people are hanging precariously on the edge of a precipice where life and death hang in the balance. There is a lot of suffering on our planet right now. For others this is a time of spiritual revelation and awakening. It is very important for each of us to give some attention to physical detoxification. We need to eat well, keep active, drink lots of pure water, do our spiritual practices, and keep the body, mind, and heart clear of toxins and negativity. Each of us is being tested, purified, and challenged to act on behalf of planetary healing. Above all, we must strive to be in alignment with our spiritual destiny and to fulfill the *dharma*, the life path and the mode of world service that is revealed to us. Thanks to astrology, we are each provided with detailed instructions.

Astrological symbols help us understand the various faculties and levels of consciousness that we activate and coordinate to become fully awakened human beings. Enthusiastically seeking to fulfill our planetary instructions, we fulfill the tasks that life asks of us, shouldering our responsibilities, and gradually manifesting our talents, our creativity, our visions. This is the path of astrological yoga.

3

The Technique of Symbol Amplification in Astrological Counseling

A skill that is central to effective astrological counseling or self-guidance is the ability to amplify chart symbols to discover their many possible meanings, just as one amplifies the imagery of a dream. Symbol amplification enables us to unfold the fullest meaning of chart symbols, and it increases our ability to use astrological knowledge to transform our lives. Before getting into the specifics, I want to talk briefly about two dimensions of astrology, the oracular, prognostic facets of astrology and the interpretive process, which makes astrology an alchemical discipline that can transform our consciousness.

The first astrological chart reading I ever had was from Chakrapani Ullal in Bombay in 1978, and it was intensely psychic. Chakrapani looked at my chart for a few minutes, then set it on the table and let his eyes turn upward toward the ceiling. His eyes shone with an intense radiance. He told me about my father's life, his injury in World War II, the obstacles he had overcome in life, about my mother's personality, her recent shoulder injury in a car crash, and the fact that her vision was much weaker in her left eye than in her right eye. He told me about my sister's recent progress in career and her upcoming marriage.

I am sure most of these insights did not come from the chart but from Chakrapani's inner vision. Chakrapani is exceptional. He is a highly evolved yogi who has practiced meditation all his life. I have often said that someone like him is clear enough in his consciousness that he could do good readings by reading tea leaves, the migration pattern of birds, or the entrails of a sheep![60]

Most astrologers do not have this kind of clairvoyance. We are not this clear or this accurate. We may make dramatic predictions, and these may be delivered with great certitude, but our pronouncements often lack subtlety and accuracy. We may lapse into simplistic statements such as saying that because someone has transiting Pluto conjunct Sun he or she will die; or that because transiting Uranus is square Venus the person will surely get a divorce.

Part of the problem is that we think we have to be psychic to be effective astrologers. Of course, it doesn't hurt; but it is not necessary, nor even one of the most essential components in the successful study and practice of astrology. What is more important is an *interpretive curiosity*, the ability to chew over and digest thoroughly the *many* possible implications of any natal placement, transit, or progression. In the practice of symbol amplification we acknowledge that there is no one correct interpretation of any astrological placement or symbol, and we entertain numerous interpretations of every planetary symbol, continuously asking *"What else could this mean?"* We dwell with the symbol and allow new meanings to disclose themselves. In this process, we feel that we are tapping into a deeper intuitive wisdom, and the spirit of guidance is felt tangibly in the astrologer's consulting room. This is how to open the eye of wisdom, how to become more clairvoyant, more clear-seeing. Moreover, this approach breaks through the fear and negativism that often creep into celestial studies, so that astrology becomes *the fearless contemplation of change.*

Sometimes astrology fosters a passive resignation that weakens our will, our creativity, our power. I have a friend whom I will call Ann who is a longtime astrologer, and, in the entire time I've known her, I've never heard her speak of her own planetary transits in positive or hopeful terms. It is always: "I'm having this awful Pluto transit," or "Maybe everything will be better when Saturn gets away from my Sun." It's interesting to me how Ann's life never changes. She never has any positive new love relationships, she lives in the same cramped apartment even though she constantly complains about it, and her career and finances are always a shambles. In a way it might be better if she didn't study astrology at all, because it does not seem to be working for her as a life path. Astrology should be the most pragmatic of disciplines, leading to tangible improvements in our quality of living. If your life doesn't change, why study astrology?

By studying astrology we gain insight into the way things *are*, the impersonal cycles and the personal developmental challenges we all face. But we also use the birthmap to *imagine possibilities*. What if transiting Saturn aspecting my Sun means that I can focus my efforts and achieve my goals? I received my professional license as a Marriage and Family Therapist when transiting Saturn was conjunct my Sun. Maybe a transit such as this is not a symbol of doom and gloom.

In *Astrology and Spiritual Awakening,* I call the kind of attitude Ann exhibits the *astrology of dread.* It is an approach to astrology where we feel doomed or trapped in an undesirable fate indicated by planetary symbols. It characterized early humanity's attempts to discern the cosmic will through the messages of the planets, and to submit consciously to this will. But in modern, post-Rudhyarian astrology we are influenced by the humanistic attitude, the understanding that we human beings have the power to au-thor our lives, to create our own destiny, and to improve our life conditions through our own efforts. The humanistic attitude is essential to an astrology that guides and facilitates our evolutionary unfoldment.

As astrologers we seek to live in alignment with universal rhythms, with curiosity about the intentions of the universe. We learn to follow our planetary instructions, whatever we discern them to be. And we need to con-template the possibilities of those instructions fully, beyond fear. A woman named Amanda told me, "I am living in the house with my husband like we are strangers. Do you think we will get divorced?" (Chart #24). This is the

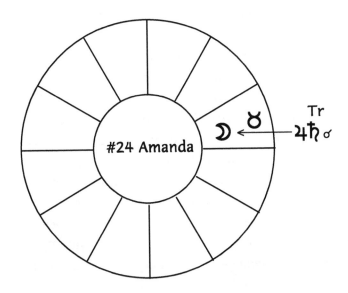

typical way people approach astrology, to get prognostic information; they consult astrology like an oracle: What will happen? What do the stars say? I noted that the upcoming Jupiter-Saturn conjunction was going to fall in Amanda's 7th house, conjunct her natal Moon at 22 Taurus. I suggested that she and her husband consider going to couples therapy if they wish to see some improvement in their marriage. They need to do some work on their relationship (transiting Saturn in 7th). She needed to express her feelings to her husband and to be more attentive to his feelings (Moon in 7th). Perhaps they could become more nurturing of one another and grow closer emotionally. It is always up to us what we will do with the transit, whether or not we will seize it as an opportunity to grow and move forward. It is not so much a matter of predicting, "What do the stars say?" Humanistic astrology is a process of imagining possibilities that could realistically unfold in resonance with the cosmic intention, such as envisioning an improved marital bond or increased income, and then taking appropriate steps to achieve those ends. Astrology is a guide to action and effort, not a substitute for them.

Symbol Amplification in Dreams and Birth Chart Interpretation

Symbol amplification is a key to translating the humanistic attitude into our astrological practice. This technique is similar to symbol amplification in dream interpretation. Dreams are multi-leveled, have multiple meanings, and are open to many possible interpretations. Ultimately, the correct interpretation of a dream is the one that resonates with the dreamer and elicits an 'Aha!' response. Dreams communicate through images, which need to be interpreted, comprehended, and grounded in application to the dreamer's current life situation. We translate the psychological meaning of dream images through *associations*. A deer may mean shyness and flightiness to one person, while to someone else it may be a symbol of innocence, or of living close to nature. A dream of a desk can evoke associations of doing one's life's work, or being trapped in one's cubicle in the workplace, or of a father or mother's desk that one recalls from childhood. According to Edward Whitmont and Sylvia Perera, a dream must be enriched through associations and amplified to the point of intelligibility.[61] Associations are any ideas, reactions, memories, or whatever else comes to mind as the dream and its images are considered. They are not necessarily rational evaluations or judgments about the images. They are utterly subjective. Associations should be explored until they reveal their emotional core and psychological significance. Only when a powerful feeling is touched may we assume that the essential core of the dream has been reached.

Specifically, the dream's meaning is derived by exploring each image in the dream, the setting, the various characters and their actions, the emotions evoked within the dream. We ask what does this image remind me of? What feelings does it bring up for me? How does this relate to my present life circumstances? What is this dream trying to teach me?

For example, a client named Sara had a dream about a rat. Her first reaction was that she was disgusted by this image, and afraid that it represented a sickness or bitterness growing inside her. I asked her what a rat reminded her of, and she said it reminded her of lawyers, and that she was now dealing with several lawyers in a dispute regarding copyright infringement and needed to find her own attorney to represent her in this matter. The rat reminded her of how tired she was of fighting these people. Sara said that the other side's lawyer had been trying to make her feel guilty for standing up for her rights. She felt like she must be a rat because she was defending her rights and speaking up in her own behalf, as if this was a sign of terrible egotism and bad character. As Sara reflected further on the image of the rat, she suddenly had a memory of being nine years old and biting her brother when he tried to molest her. She said, "He never bothered me again after that." Now she saw that the rat was a positive symbol of her capacity to protect herself, to use her teeth when necessary. Sara put a little toy stuffed rat on her altar, and began to honor the inner wisdom that it represents for her. The rat became a spirit totem, an ally and a healer for her.

So it is with symbol amplification in birth chart interpretation. We note our associations to each planetary placement or symbol and we ask ourselves what emotional responses are evoked by it. What does this remind me of about my life, my goals, my struggles? What does this say about where I am, where I'm going, and what I need to do now to get there? What is this trying to teach me? Often the chart symbols we are most afraid of and that evoke the most fear and dread—in other words, the planetary aspects or transits

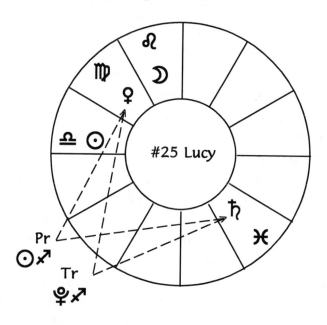

that are metaphorically like the rat dream—are the ones that have the most to teach us.

For example, a 65-year-old woman named Lucy felt disappointed that she had not achieved more in her life, having spent many years as a housewife raising her children (Chart #25). Lucy had a lot of concern about the meaning of her natal Saturn in Pisces in the 5th house. Did it mean something bad about her children, she asked? I said, "It means that your children have been the focal point of your adult life, and that you have devoted yourself to them selflessly." She said, "Yes, I have great kids. I taught them well. I was a great educator. They have good values, good moral principles." I pointed out her natal Jupiter conjunct the Ascendant, symbol of a teacher. Next we examined Lucy's natal Moon in Leo at the Midheaven. Lucy had read in a book that this meant she was very egotistical and needed a lot of attention. I brought her attention to the Moon as a symbol of mother and motherhood. It had been her evolutionary goal to fully live the archetype of mother, to be a mother of joy (Moon in Leo). She was, in fact, immensely proud of her children and delighted by them. Indeed, it seemed that Moon conjunct her Midheaven suggested that becoming a mother was the *pinnacle* of her evolution. She said, "For years I have been interested in the Moon Goddess, the religion of the great Mother. Mother is the beginning of all things, it is the primary archetype. And I have lived that, I am that Mother." As she said this, her face exuded great contentment. In that moment it seemed that all sense of failure or lack of achievement was being dissolved. This is the kind of healing that can occur through the study of astrology.

Lucy had natal Venus opposite Saturn. She told me that she had read that this aspect meant she would be unhappy or rejected in love and that she couldn't open her heart. Yet she had been married to the same man for forty three years. I asked her to consider that this aspect could be viewed as a symbol of long-term, sustained, mature love. She had learned to live a real human being. This is the lesson: to love *this* flawed, real person. That is maturity in love. That is the *secret* of love!

Transiting Pluto was currently squaring Lucy's natal Venus in the 11th opposite natal Saturn. I will confess that my own initial instinct when I see transiting Pluto aspecting Saturn is often to imagine some severe stressor or adversity, a difficult period. But maybe it could mean much more. Lucy reported that during this transit both of her children got married (Venus is in the 7th house from the child-5th: her children's relationships), and both became parents themselves. One meaning of transiting Pluto square Saturn in the 5th was that her children were assuming the responsibilities of parenthood. They were becoming more serious about their lives. Openness to new dimensions of meaning in Lucy's chart symbols revealed much constructive purpose at work in her life.

Lucy also had the progressed Sun square Saturn, an aspect that traditional texts might lead us to view as a symbol of struggles, suffering, adversity, and misfortune. She said, "That's bad, isn't it?" I spoke in general terms about how this progression often suggests a need to adjust to changes related to growing older. I asked for her associations to this statement; was it meaningful to her now? As it turned out, Lucy was actively seeking to develop her awareness about aging. She was doing research on aging, studying the life cycle, and helping others in her age group live better, and cope with changes in their bodies and their social status. This is an inspiring expression of progressed Sun square Saturn. Lucy was able to see that this aspect need not be a symbol of suffering, that it represented a developmental project she had already embraced, and that indeed the Sun-Saturn progression had a

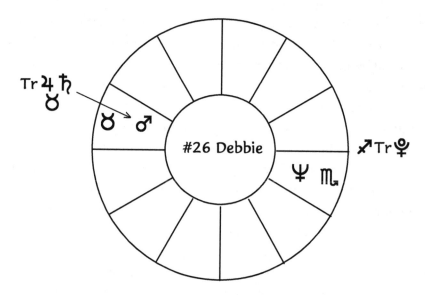

positive intention and meaning for her. This is the kind of understanding we gain by amplifying planetary symbols.

A woman named Debbie with transiting Pluto conjunct the Descendant met a powerful and influential man and fell in love with him (Chart #26). She had been dating another man who now became violently jealous. Debbie feared for her safety and had to go to court to get a restraining order placed on him. Debbie had been studying astrology and was quite concerned about transiting the Jupiter-Saturn conjunction in her 12th house conjunct Mars and opposite Neptune. She'd read books suggesting she might be lonely, institutionalized, or hospitalized. Did it mean something bad was going to happen to her because she had left this other man? Was it karmically destined that she was going to come under attack (Saturn conjunct Mars in the 12th house of karma)? I interpreted the chart symbols differently, noting her keen interests in spirituality and metaphysics and astrology and asking if she was developing new interests in yoga and enlightened sexuality (Mars-Neptune). Debbie confirmed all this, talking excitedly about her yoga classes and recent Tantra workshops, and how she had been studying astrology feverishly. She was about to leave her job to help her new husband run his professional practice—a role in which she would be in the background yet could devote herself to her contemplative interests and pursuits (12th house). I asked Debbie if, with Jupiter-Saturn in her 12th house, she felt that she was dedicating her life to a higher purpose. Yes, she responded. She felt she

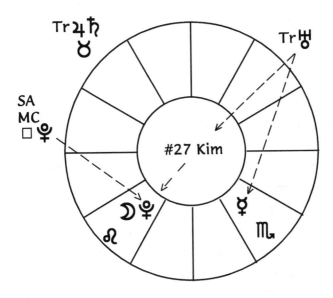

was being guided to new areas of spiritual awareness and service to humanity. With transiting Jupiter-Saturn opposite natal Neptune in her 6th house of health, Debbie was learning the principles of homeopathy, vibrational healing and subtle energy medicine, as well as studying medical astrology. Moreover, Debbie was pregnant, and Jupiter-Saturn in the 12th became an instruction to go deeply into a peaceful cocoon of tranquility, meditation, and sleep during her pregnancy. There were multiple, growthful layers of meaning in this transit, waiting to be unfolded through amplification.

Kim, the mother of two children, had solar arc MC square natal Pluto, and her progressed Moon was in Scorpio (Chart #27). She also had transiting Uranus beginning a two year opposition to natal Moon, square natal Mercury in Scorpio in the 5th house. She reported that her sixteen-year-old daughter, Pam, had started talking trash, cussing, talking sassy to her, and that she constantly had sex on the brain (Mercury in 5th house in Scorpio). She said, "Is this what I have to look forward to for the next two years? I asked my friend who is an astrologer about this and she said Uranus opposite Moon means emotional upset or disturbance in the home. Are my kids going to keep acting weird and become totally uncontrollable?" I asked Kim to consider what the transit might have to teach her, what the *intention* of the transit might be. I noted that the Moon was the symbol of motherhood and her own feelings about motherhood. I described how Uranus represents an urge toward freedom, liberation. Perhaps the transit was communicating that she needed to change her approach to parenting, to become less rigid, more open-minded, less uptight. Yes, she said. "Pam wants to explore her sexuality and I have to accept this." I replied, "Clearly Pam wants more freedom, more independence. But maybe the transit also means that you need more freedom, too." Kim said, "I'd like my husband and kids to take care of themselves more so I can be more independent." We also noted the recent transiting Jupiter-Saturn conjunction in Kim's 11th house, the 7th house from the child-5th. It was perfectly appropriate that her teenage daughter was becoming more interested in developing relationships with boys.

I noted that Kim's Leo Moon was placed in the 2nd house. Money was really not an issue in her life; her husband took very good care of her financially. So what further level of meaning could this transit hold for her? It occurred to me that the 2nd house is also the 10th house from the child-5th. I asked if her children were undergoing any changes in their career plans or goals. Yes, she replied. Her twenty-four-year-old son John had been facing major challenges in beginning his career. John repeatedly stormed off of job sites, and always seemed to have problems with bosses. He seemed to be grappling with a streak of narcissism, a feeling that he is special and should be given special treatment (Leo). He would become enraged when he felt slighted or his pride was wounded. Kim and I discussed ways she could nurturingly encourage him to be aware of these tendencies and to prove himself capable and worthy of career advancement by demonstrating his natural talents, abilities, and inner radiance.

Symbol Amplification Through Derived House Analysis

This last example illustrates that one important way of amplifying planetary symbolism is through *derived house analysis*. This method can be especially helpful in illuminating the complex web of our varied human relationships. For example, if the 1st house represents self and personal identity and the 4th house is my family, then issues pertaining to my spouse's family are found by examining the 10th house, which is the 4th house from the partner-7th. Similarly, the 4th house is the 10th house from the 7th and thus rules the spouse's career. A man named Philip, who had Jupiter pass through the 4th house conjunct his natal Sun, reported that his wife's career advanced through an unexpected promotion. The partner's finances are ruled by the 8th house, which is the money-2nd from the 7th. A woman reported that when transiting Neptune passed into her 8th house her husband's finances fell apart; his financial situation remained tenuous until transiting Jupiter passed through the 8th house. A man with Saturn in Sagittarius in his 3rd house, conjunct Mars, ruler of his 2nd house (money) spent a lot of money paying for his wife to go to graduate school. The 3rd house is the education-9th house from the partner-7th; therefore it rules his wife's higher education.

An important area of concern for many parents is their children's relationships and social life. This is illumined by examining the 11th house, which is the 7th house from the child-5th, thus governing a child's relationships. For example, a man named Robert reported that his daughter met a new boyfriend who showed serious interest in marriage and whose career prospects were quite sparkling when transiting Saturn was conjunct natal Jupiter in Robert's 11th house. His daughter's relationship and eventual marriage to this man were very positive.

Perhaps the most dramatic recent example of derived house analysis I've seen recently concerned a woman named Louise who had solar arc Pluto in Libra in the 11th house opposite her natal Sun in Aries in the 5th house (Chart #28). I asked if her child (5th house Sun) had recently had any dis-

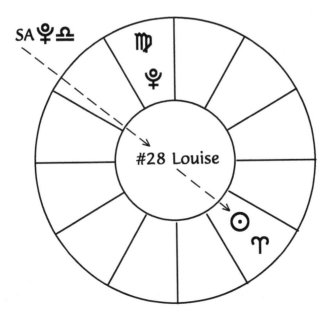

turbing experiences involving violence or crime (Pluto), possibly through his relationship with other children (11th house). She replied that her son had accidentally shot another boy with a gun that the boy had brought to school. The boy lived and made a full recovery. Louise's son was deeply affected by this traumatic experience and underwent a profound transformation, recognizing the preciousness and impermanence of life, and of friendship.

Openness to Multiple Levels of Meaning

This last example involving Pluto reminds us that amplification is important and necessary because certain planetary symbols can manifest in such

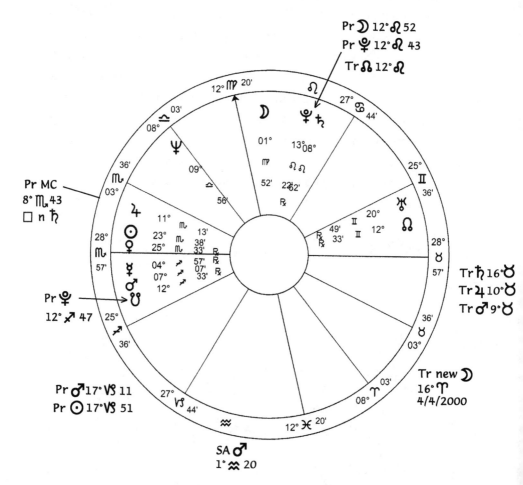

Chart #29 Terrence McKenna
Natal chart with transits/progressions for date of death April 3, 2000

widely varying ways. A purely prognostic, oracular approach often will not work because the symbolism is so rich and complex. Let us look at several more examples involving Pluto. Sometimes Pluto can be death symbolism, pure and simple, and no amount of symbol amplification can change this fact. Terrence McKenna (Chart #29)(born Nov 16, 1946, 7:25 am MST, Paonia, Colorado) died of a brain tumor when his progressed Moon (12 Leo 52) was in exact conjunction with natal Pluto (13 Leo 22) and progressed Pluto (12 Leo 43); and while transiting Pluto (12 Sag 47) was closely conjunct his south node (12 Sag 32) in the first house (which rules the head). Pluto rules cancer and tumors. Terrence also had a progressed conjunction of Sun-Mars, Mars being the co-ruler of his natal Scorpio Ascendant, and dispositor of his natal Sun in Scorpio (traditionally the sign of death). For the record, he also had Naibod progressed MC at 8 Scorpio 43 closely squaring natal Saturn (8 Leo 52). Solar arc Mars (1 Aquarius 20) was tightly quincunx his natal Moon (1 Virgo 51).

But we should not anticipate death every time we see a strong Pluto transit. In many instances Pluto manifests as experiences of interpersonal intensities, disagreements, or hostilities. A woman with transiting Pluto conjunct Mars in Sagittarius on the Descendant had a huge power struggle and disagreement with her husband about their child's education. The 7th house is the education-3rd from the child-5th. Also, she had much stress related to her child's transportation to and from school (3rd house from 5th). Her husband was verbally abusive during this transit.

Pluto can also suggest the meaning of an ordeal that is ultimately regenerative. A married man named Ron had an affair while transiting Pluto was conjunct his natal Venus in the 7th house of marriage (Chart #30). He felt tremendous guilt about this. Our discussion of Pluto aspecting Venus helped Ron see that while he felt regret, he also secretly felt joy that he had lived fully, even living this moment of transgression against his marital commitment, in violation of the Saturnian laws of the social order. He said he felt a sense of wholeness. He had lived his shadow side; he had experienced forbidden pleasures. He had inflicted pain on his wife, too. But what was most important was how this experience could be a catalyst of personal change. Sometimes the encounter with our dark side (or that of others) strengthens our resolve to improve our character. He needed to accept that this moment

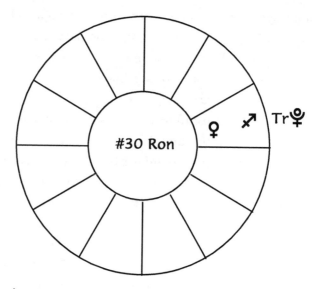

was over. Pluto's pass over Venus was complete. Remarkably, his wife was able to let go of the past and move forward. Ultimately, the depth and purity of her love in the face of betrayal became evident to him, and—through struggle, catharsis, and reconciliation—their relationship was transformed. He was in a new phase of his life defined by transiting Jupiter-Saturn in his first house, opposite Venus. He wants to be more upright and ethical and to fulfill his commitments. He does not need to castigate himself endlessly; he needs to change his actions. He had his moment to cross over the line and it was over and finished. In this example, we see that the emotional, psychological, relational, and spiritual depth and complexity of the process symbolized by the Pluto transit could not be encompassed through a simple statement about a marital crisis.

Pluto also represents catharsis and clearing of poisonous emotions. A few years ago someone broke into my house and stole some valuables on the day of an exact Mars-Pluto square, and while my progressed Midheaven was exactly conjunct natal Pluto. I was quite upset and angry about the burglary but I didn't want to hold onto these feelings. As I contemplated the possible meaning of this event in the light of these planetary symbols, I began to read a Buddhist text called Eight Verses for Training the Mind, with the Dalai Lama's commentaries.[62] The text is about removing psychological impediments to an enlightened attitude. It asks us to train ourselves to be Buddhas, to consider how would the Buddha act in this situation? The text reads: "When I see beings of a wicked nature, oppressed by violent misdeeds and afflictions, may I hold them dear as if I had found a rare and precious treasure." The Dalai Lama says, "Some people, when they see others who are exhausted by sufferings and oppressed by delusions, tend to avoid these experiences because they are afraid of getting involved and carried away. Boddhisattvas, instead of avoiding such situations, face them bravely as an opportunity to bring happiness to other sentient beings."[63] The text continues, "When others out of envy treat me badly with slander, abuse, and the like, may I suffer the loss and offer the victory to them." The Dalai Lama says,

> When other beings, especially those who hold a grudge against you, abuse and harm you out of envy, you should not abandon them, but hold them as objects of your greatest compassion and take care of them. Thus, the practitioner should take the 'loss' on himself or herself, and offer the 'victory' to others. Practitioners of the mind of enlightenment take the loss on themselves and offer the victory to others, not with the motivation to become virtuous themselves but rather with the motivation to help other sentient beings. . . A person who harms you should be seen not only as someone who needs your special care, but also as someone who is your spiritual guide. You will find that your enemy is your supreme teacher.[64]

It is up to us to view our Plutonian tests, crises, and initiations in this way—as opportunities for the practice of altruism and the refinement of our character. These deeper levels of meaning in a Plutonian process come to light when we amplify planetary symbols. We cannot simply rely on our psychic abilities. What matters is what we make of our life situations, what consciousness we bring to them. We go beyond the astrology of events and prediction, to discover the deeper core of meaning implicit in events, their implicit *intention* and perfect design. It is in this way that astrology truly begins to serve the transformation of our consciousness.

Symbol Amplification and Chart Rectification

Another way to practice symbol amplification is through chart rectification. Here is an example of how I rectified the chart of Phyllis, a woman in her fifties (Chart #31). To rectify a chart I ask clients a variety of questions: Have they ever been married, and when? Do they have any children? Siblings? What was their family of origin like? What is their occupation? Then I try to find correlations with natal chart symbols. Also, the timing of significant

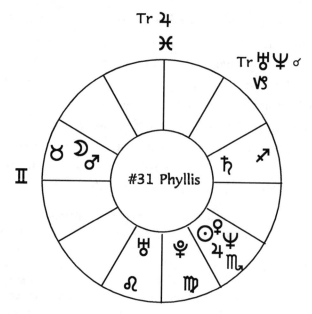

events should be indicated by appropriate transits. Phyllis had no idea at all what time she was born, so to determine the correct birth time I tried out various arrangements and house placements of her birth planets to find the chart that matched her life.

The first thing Phyllis told me that was relevant was that she had been in three relationships in her life, all long-term, all with men at least ten years older than herself. I arranged the chart angles so that Saturn was placed in the 7th house. She said, "My husband was a cold person, mechanical; he never showed his emotions. He was not warm." She described her current boyfriend as "very reliable, hard-working; we have a very stable relationship." Saturn in the 7th house seemed to aptly represent these relationships. This chart placed Pluto in the 4th house. Phyllis had been adopted (Pluto in 4th). She reported a history of family violence. "My adopted parents divorced and my mom married a man who was crazy, violent. "Both my parents were mean alcoholics," she said. Uranus was in the 3rd house of the tentative rectified chart. Were her siblings in any way unusual, unconventional, or strange, I asked. She said, "All my siblings are weird, crazy, all of them are on Prozac." This chart put the Sun, Venus, Jupiter, and Neptune in Phyllis' 5th house. She said she likes to party, drink, smoke pot, go to bars (Sun-Neptune, 5th house focus). In 1993, the Uranus-Neptune conjunction had fallen in the 8th house of the tentative rectified chart. I asked if there had been any unexpected developments regarding joint finances, inheritance. Phyllis said, "I unexpectedly inherited a lot of money. My husband and I were about to get a divorce and he got really weird and wanted the money to be joint property, but legally he wasn't entitled to it. We had many disagreements about money in that period. The divorce settlement was very complicated." So far, this rectified chart seemed accurate to me. It placed Moon-Mars conjunction in her 12th house. I asked Phyllis if she tended to hide a lot of angry feelings. She said, "I hold them all inside. I'm working on that in therapy." I became more convinced the rectified chart was correct when I asked her about career developments on a particular recent date when Jupiter had passed over her MC. She replied, "I quit my job and they offered me six months severance pay as a way of showing appreciation for all my hard work."

Now I ask you to practice amplification of your own chart symbols. Breathe for a few moments. Identify a natal planetary placement, or aspect, or some current transit. Pause and consider the possible meaning and intention of this symbol. Amplify the symbol, name your associations to it, your emotional response, your fears about it, your sense of the possibilities it holds for you. Use derived house analysis to illuminate other levels of meaning you might not have noticed at first glance. Through the technique of symbol amplification, chart interpretation becomes a form of deep meditation revealing infinite meanings.

4

Astrology as a Spiritual Practice

Astrology is a wisdom teaching that guides us toward a spiritually illumined existence. It is a rigorous training for perfection, which, over time, instills in us qualities of spiritual maturity, such as discernment, humor, steadiness in times of suffering, and expanded capacity to love. In this chapter I present some further case examples to illustrate these points. We will observe again how meditation and a quiet mind enhance our capacity to unfold the deepest potentials of every planetary placement, every transit and progression.

Astrology is much vaster than we think it is when we begin our studies. It is more than just a way to gain material advantage through foreknowledge of planetary cycles—although it is certainly that. It is also a spiritual practice, a training for wholeness, a life-long course in consciousness.

What do I mean when I say astrology is a spiritual practice? I mean that its purpose is not only to predict events but to help us live a spiritually illumined existence, to center us fully in the present moment, and to awaken in us the power and wisdom to meet all of life's challenges effectively and wisely. Also, astrology is a spiritual *practice*, one that ripens with time and experience, yes, with practice. It expands our consciousness.

Astrology is a spiritual practice that awakens in us enlightened spiritual qualities such as *discernment, courage* (heart), and a sense of *humor* and appreciation of divine mystery and perfection. We develop growing powers of discernment through the contemplative discipline of astrology. We learn from our mistakes of judgment, our tendency to be too pessimistic or too optimistic in our assessment of the possible outcomes of some upcoming transit. For example, we wonder, "Will I fall in love when transiting Venus is conjunct my Descendant?" Probably this rapid and rather soft transit is not enough in itself to bring this outcome. But solar arc Venus conjunct

Descendant, or a transiting Jupiter-Saturn conjunction on the Descendant, in the 7th house, very well might have this outcome. So, we learn to make discerning judgements about the relative strength and length of various planetary contacts. Solar arc Venus conjunct Descendant has a longer and stronger impact than transiting Venus conjunct Descendant.

As we develop discernment, our interpretations become subtler and more realistic. We learn not to expect disaster every time the transiting Moon is conjunct natal Saturn or even when transiting Saturn is conjunct natal Moon; but we do realistically anticipate the more stressful effects of a transit such as Mars conjunct or square natal Saturn. I have natal Saturn in the 3rd house (which, among other meanings, has rulership over mobility, transportation, and motor vehicles), and I can generally anticipate when I will have car trouble. It almost always happens when transiting Mars is conjunct, square, or opposite natal Saturn in the 3rd.

We also learn to properly estimate the power and potential of planetary transits. Grant, a man who had been trying to make money as a self-employed, independent consultant, had a Mars-Jupiter-Saturn conjunction in Taurus forming in his 6th house (Chart #32). For two years I told him that by the time of this conjunction he had a good chance to find a better-paying job (Jupiter-Saturn in Taurus in 6th house). Grant ignored me completely until the month of the triple conjunction; he really didn't think much would

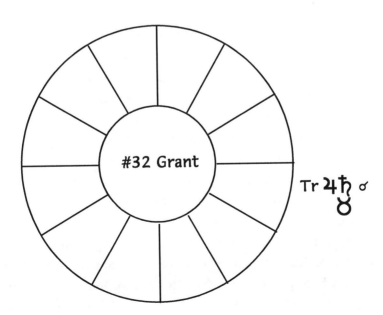

#32 Grant

Tr ♃♄ ♂
♉

happen. In March, 2000, when Mars entered Taurus along with Jupiter and Saturn, he spontaneously started to circulate his resume, had several excellent offers, and by the week of the exact Jupiter-Saturn conjunction he began a job at twice his previous salary. This is one of most exciting aspects of astrology—that we can maximize our potentials for success by doing things at the right time, when the moment is truly ripe.

Strategically Timed Action

Astrology teaches us the art of *strategically timed action.* We figure out when is or is not a good time to ask someone out on a date, or to try to change jobs, or to change residences. I had been planning to move to a new apartment for over a year but I kept delaying until transiting Jupiter passed over my 4th house cusp and several planets in my 4th house. When that transit happened I found a great rental home the first day I went out looking.

Celestial insights can help us make good decisions about housing and real estate, parenting children, education, job changes, relationships with others. When I had my Saturn return in the 3rd house and I went back to graduate school I was ready for the challenge that awaited me, even though I knew it would be years before I would see the rewards of my efforts. At that moment, the cosmos asked me to learn, to acquire knowledge (3rd house). Years later (in 2000), during a conjunction of Sun, Mercury, Venus, and Mars in Cancer, I found a beautiful home and bought it (Cancer rules homes and real estate). At around the same time, transiting Jupiter-Saturn came into conjunction in my 8th house and I was able to get the financing to make it possible. I moved forward, embracing the yoga of debt. Developmentally, I was ready to buy a house, and to take on a mortgage. I was ready for this new responsibility. We begin to want what the universe wants of us, as best we can discern this. We want to do what life asks of us. We become disciples of the cosmos, striving to fulfill our celestial instructions to the best of our abilities. We begin to perceive our transits and progressions as a set of lessons, revealing the portals we need to pass through to proceed on our evolutionary journeys.

Here is another story about the practical significance of astrology. A woman named Linda had a ten-year-old son named David who was evaluated by a school psychologist for Attention Deficit Hyperactivity Disorder

(ADHD). He was bored and restless in school, constantly daydreaming, and had difficulty paying attention in class. The psychologist wanted to put David on Ritalin, a drug that is widely prescribed but may have some serious side effects.[65] Linda consulted me about David's chart. He was in the middle of progressed Sun square Neptune. "He just wants to stay home and watch television and play Dungeons and Dragons. His fantasy life is amazing." After discussing with me the kinds of experiences that are common under the symbolism of Neptune (spaciness, inward directed focus, lack of focus on practical tasks, heightened powers of imagination), Linda decided to allow David to stay home from school, rather than forcing him to conform to social norms and behavioral expectations. After a few weeks of freedom David was satiated and ready to return to school, where he began to get good grades and to channel his imagination into writing stories and study-ing mythology, dinosaurs, whales, sharks, and dolphins (Neptune: creatures of the ocean). Astrological symbolism convinced Linda that the ADHD label did not accurately describe her son, and that she did not need to put her son on Ritalin. She became clearer that there was nothing fundamentally or constitutionally wrong with David; in fact, he was unusually creative and intelligent—and intuitive.

We are not victims of the planetary patterns. Rather, we are instructed by them. Andrea had natal Mars and Pluto conjunct in her 6th house (Chart

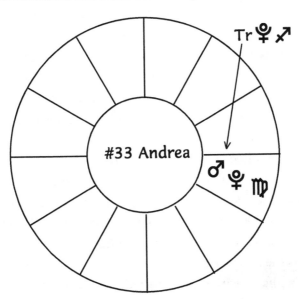

#33). While transiting Pluto was square natal Mars-Pluto, she felt bullied at work by a vindictive, controlling, domineering co-worker (Pluto in 6th house) whom she felt pushed around everyone in the office. Finally, Andrea stood up to this woman firmly, and told her off in a way that no one else had the courage to do. Rather than viewing this episode just as an eruption of negativity in the workplace (though that was true, too), Andrea was able to view it as an initiation into greater strength and assertiveness. The transit corresponded to an awakening of her Mars-Pluto power. She realized that no one has the right to violate her; she learned to stand up for herself. The transit had achieved its purpose.

Reflection on astrological symbolism also awakens our sense of *humor*. Sometimes the correspondence of transits with events is quite funny. At one point I had been single for a while and became somewhat grouchy and jaded about love. I was sitting around my apartment in my underwear poring over the ephemeris. Transiting Saturn was conjunct Venus, transiting Uranus was conjunct the Venus-Mars midpoint, the progressed Moon was in my 7th house, and transiting Venus and Juno were conjunct my Descendant at that very moment. I thought to myself, "Hmph, astrology doesn't work! I should be involved in some kind of a relationship. But there is nothing in sight." At that moment the phone rang. It was an ex-girlfriend, who seemed very interested in getting together with me. Our relationship was rekindled in that moment. Diana and I are still together, years later! On another note, when transiting Pluto went stationary direct aspecting my Midheaven a sewer exploded, spewing sewage all over my yard. When I had solar arc Uranus conjunct my Mars-Pluto midpoint I was peacefully weeding my garden when I was suddenly attacked by a swarm of bees. I got multiple stings, went into shock, had a near-death experience, and ended up in the hospital. This wasn't all that funny at the time, but when I saw this event in the light of planetary symbolism I was struck at how comical the correlation was. Ebertin wrote this about Uranus=Mars/Pluto: "cruelty, violence, brutality, sudden disasters or calamities of great consequence."[66] Better to exhaust the karma of this solar arc contact through bee stings than through injury, act of violence, or a major blowout with a friend or colleague.

Sometimes the correspondence of both inner and outer events with planetary symbols fills us with awe and gratitude. While Neptune was conjunct

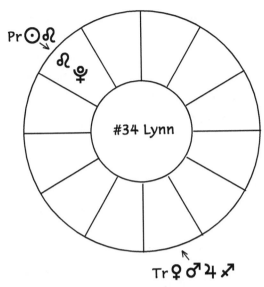

my Moon, at a moment of deep reconciliation with myself after a period of personal failure and disappointment (discussed in Chapter 2) I had the following dream: "I am at a local bookstore on a Sunday afternoon. People have gathered and are standing in rows waste deep in water, while among them a few individuals are experiencing a ritual immersion in the water. I am one of those undergoing this spiritual cleansing and baptism. The water is clear and soft. I am renewed through this immersion in the restorative waters. I am whole again." I couldn't have asked for a more perfect Neptunian healing experience at that moment of my life.

Astrological studies teach us humility, as well as trust in the inscrutable intelligence of the divine order. Once, while doing a yearly update for a client named Lynn (Chart #34), I noted that she was soon going to have a transiting conjunction of Venus, Mars, and Jupiter in her 4th house, which I thought might indicate that she would move or beautify her home, and that this time could mark the start of a new relationship, or setting up a household with someone. Lynn assured me that moving was out of the question as she loved her current home. She had been single for many years, and there were currently no romantic prospects. I also noted that Lynn's progressed Sun was closely conjunct natal Pluto in the 11th house, but I wasn't clear how that might relate to the possibilities indicated by the transiting conjunction in her 4th house. At the exact time of the Venus-Mars-Jupiter conjunction, Lynn's home burned to the ground in a major fire that destroyed her entire neighborhood (Sun-Pluto in 11th house), and she moved in with a longtime Platonic male friend. They were married a year later. She told me that the one thing that helped her bear the grief of losing her home and all her material possessions was the knowledge that at that time she was meant to begin a new phase of domestic life in love and partnership. In the light of this planetary symbolism, the crisis of losing her house seemed to serve a deeper purpose.

Conscious Suffering

Astrology is like an invisible mentor, ever available to guide and reveal the light in all circumstances. It calms and centers us in times of emotional upset. Celestial studies instill in us *courage* to face difficulties with equanimity and open eyes. We learn to find renewal through consciously experiencing life's inevitable moments of suffering. A woman named Tricia sat with her husband while he died of cancer, while transiting Pluto in Scorpio was conjunct her natal Saturn in Scorpio at the Midheaven, exactly quincunx natal Venus in Gemini (Chart #35). It was a time of grief, loss, inner strength. For her, Saturn in Scorpio at the Midheaven meant that mastering the fear of death, facing it with courage, strength, and maturity, was one of her highest evolutionary achievements in this lifetime. Tricia learned that death is a part of life. We may pass through dark sections of the forest, yet with astrology as our guide there is always light on the Path.

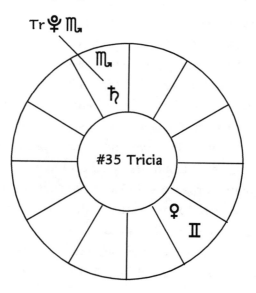

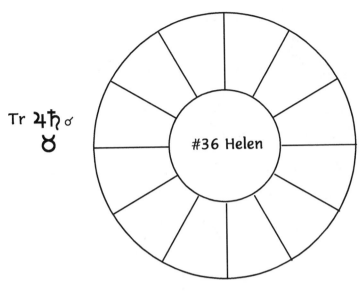

Tr ♃♄♂
♉
#36 Helen

The ability to transform our suffering through reflection on planetary symbols is the heart of astrological alchemy. Helen, a forty-year-old woman, is having transiting Jupiter and Saturn in her 12th house (Chart #36). She has been experiencing a period of isolation and loneliness. She resists this, feeling that she ought to be in a relationship. But the universe has its own intelligence. She has been immersing herself in dreamwork, meditation, and astrology. Her birthmap and current transits are pointing the way for her to follow, which, for this moment, is the way inward. During this time of inner exploration Helen is forming a new identity as a practical metaphysician (Jupiter-Saturn in Taurus in the 12th house). Her practice of astrology is masterful, down-to-earth, and increasingly lucrative. Her face glows with peace as she surrenders and trusts that she is finding her proper place in the universe.

Astrology teaches us *patience*, the wisdom to wait for the appropriate moment for things to manifest. A seventy-year-old woman named Victoria has been single for thirty years, since her Uranus opposition at age 40–41 (Chart #37). She has waited a long time for love. She had a progressed sextile of Venus and Mars. To her amazement, an older gentleman responded to her ad in the "Personals" column, they fell in love, and soon married. As Rudhyar taught, cycles are unceasing, there is always another chance to complete our unfinished evolutionary tasks.

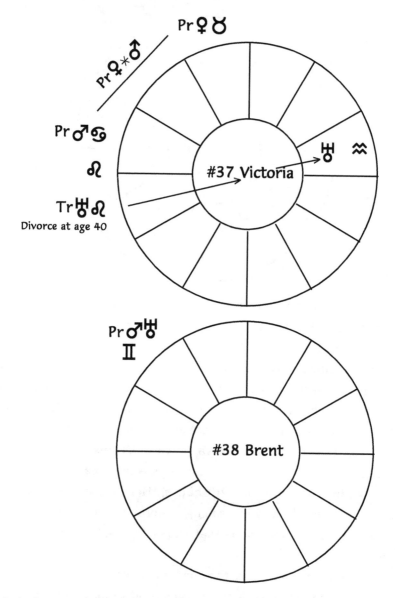

Astrology teaches us the wisdom of *letting go of the past*. A gay man named Brent had a progressed Mars-Uranus conjunction in his 11th house during the 1980s (Chart #38). He spent four or five years going to ecstatic dance parties in nightclubs where men would engage in sexual acts with multiple partners, everyone dosed on amphetamines (Mars-Uranus). Brent looked back on that time with nostalgia and a sense of loss. I said to him, "That moment is over, it will never happen again. You can be happy that you had

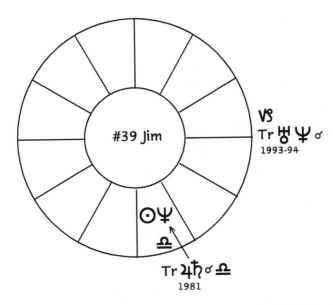

that experience, but it would be foolish to try to repeat it." This is the type of awareness we learn from astrology. It helps us get real with the truth of *this* moment, whatever its quality.

Astrology also helps us discern the meaning and evolutionary purpose of unusual states of consciousness, mystical experiences, and moments of spiritual awakening—which are often turning points in our lives, and sometimes quite tumultuous as well. A client named Jim had a natal Sun-Neptune conjunction in Libra in the 4th house (Chart #39). In 1981, when transiting Jupiter and Saturn came into conjunction in Libra (exactly conjunct his natal Sun-Neptune), Jim had the most significant experience of his life: an encounter with Christ. He said, "I saw visions of his sacrifice and love for the world. I understood the atonement. I was filled with a love that I'd never felt before. A light and power came over me. I was praying for the entire world. I also had precognitive dreams, visions, and encounters with the numinous." I asked him to contemplate the way that this experience was a discovery of his true nature (Sun-Neptune). Jim said, "This was the highest spiritual experience I ever had. And it has been agonizing for me that I can't get back to it; I can't recover the power of that moment no matter how much I pray and meditate." I replied, "Why do you need to repeat it? This was an experience that had a permanent effect on your consciousness. You discovered the purpose of your life—to live that consciousness, that love that was revealed to you. You have pursued a spiritual life since that time. The experience achieved its purpose. Your task is to live your whole life in the light of that experience, and in remembrance of it."

Astrology helps us find meaning and orientation during our most chaotic periods of life. In 1992, Jim faced a great challenge. Transiting Uranus and Neptune were conjunct right on his Descendant. Jim had several spiritual experiences that led him to explore a polygamous lifestyle. He said, "I tried to establish a life with a second woman and her children. I was excommunicated from my Church, I lost my job. It was devastating. I almost lost my family. Then Spirit guided me to go back to my wife. There was a lot of woundedness in our marriage. It took a long time for us to rebuild our relationship. But miraculously, she forgave me and we've been healing our life together." It's not the astrologer's role to pass judgement so I discussed these events with Jim dispassionately, trying to understand the Uranian rebellion against societal norms and the Neptunian delusion, confusion, and poor judgement that were evident in this situation. As I considered the symbol of Uranus-Neptune conjunct Jim's Descendant, I wondered if he had truly experienced an infusion of spiritual light in the context of this monumental relational crisis. The ways of Spirit are mysterious and often stormy. Aurobindo wrote,

> In the hour of God cleanse thy soul of all self-deceit and hypocrisy and vain self-flattering that thou mayest look straight into thy spirit and hear that which summons it. . . . [B]eing pure cast aside all fear; for the hour is often terrible, a fire and a whirlwind and a tempest, a treading of the winepress of the wrath of God; but s/he who can stand up in it on the truth of his/her purpose is s/he who shall stand; even though s/he fall, s/he shall rise again; even though s/he seem to pass on the wings of the wind, s/he shall return. Nor let worldly prudence whisper too closely in thy ear; for it is the hour of the unexpected.[67]

I asked Jim to meditate deeply for a few moments and to consider what might have been the evolutionary purpose of this painful relational drama. From a deep inner space, Jim said, "I feel that to experience the fullest power of love I needed to experience love shattering the vessel of social convention. It was a period of exquisite, ecstatic agony. My life was falling apart, I was in bliss, I was shattered, all at the same time. And in the chaos I felt the presence of God and the power of grace pulling me through the darkness, enfolding me into a light transcending the ego. I came through the experience completely humbled and committed to service of the divine will." When we contemplate our chart symbols with a quiet mind, their deeper significance can be revealed spontaneously in a moment of revelation in which we feel, and know, how our suffering brings us home to grace.

Astrological Alchemy and the Formative Use of Will

Astrology can be viewed as a kind of alchemical practice because it enables us to transmute the Saturnian lead of our lives, our suffering, and our personal upheavals (the *prima materia* or base metal) into the philosopher's stone, the radiant gold of consciousness. The goal of alchemy is also to achieve the *coniunctio,* the union of opposites, King and Queen, Sun and Moon, male and female, young and old, the hero and the shadow or adversary. In Jim's case we saw the union of saint and sinner, agony and ecstasy, human confusion and divine grace.

According to Edward Edinger,[68] the alchemical *coniunctio* represents "the creation of consciousness," through the union of opposites. The practice of astrology is also conducive to the creation of consciousness—consciousness about cycles and changing seasons of life experience, consciousness of intention, consciousness of possibilities. Astrology is the ultimate alchemical discipline. [69]

Astrological symbols often resonate with stages of the alchemical work described in medieval European alchemy. For example, contacts involving natal or transiting Mars may correspond to periods when we pass through the transforming tests of *calcinatio,* transforming the fuming fire of passion and desire (as noted in Footnote 23 of this volume). A traditional symbol of the *calcinatio* is the image of a King (symbol of the ego) in a sweatbox. He's hot, sweating, being transformed through heat and fire. Transits involving Neptune correspond to the alchemical phase of *solutio,* dissolving, purification, and transformation by water. We experience ourselves melted down to a liquid state, or have dreams of bathing in a lake, ocean, or fountain; the rain of grace descends on us. We merge with all; there is no separation. Neptune is also a symbol of the alchemical phase called *sublimatio* in which we experience the rising up of Spirit, symbolized by a white bird, or by the ladder, connecting earth and heaven. In one alchemical image, the King is immersed in the waters of a fountain (*solutio*), and a white bird descends and hovers above his head (*sublimatio*) as the King's eyes turn inward and upward toward the divine light. Immersed in formless waters, our spirit rises up. Another *sublimatio* image is Dew, a gift from heaven down to earth.

Transits involving Saturn may correlate with several alchemical themes: the *nigredo* phase of blackening, dealing with suffering; and *coagulatio*, the stage of solidification, coming into form, having life structures solidify. One image of this that of an eagle chained to a toad; part of us wants to soar (*sublimatio*), but we also need to honor our need to come down to earth, to deal with ordinary, low-level reality. It is not healthy to fly off into spirituality without dealing with the body, the earth, money, and relationships, all the things that keep us grounded. Another medieval Saturn-*coagulatio* symbol is the image of a snake nailed to a cross: we are nailed, caught in matter. We have to deal with the material world to be transformed.

Transits involving Pluto may correspond to the alchemical phase of *mortificatio*, in which we confront death and mortality, and gain hope in future cycles of life. In one image, grain is growing out of a grave. We realize that death is transformation; there is a life seed within the death moment. Uranus corresponds to the alchemical phase of *separatio*: separating from parents, the collective; this is the principle of individuation. Sometimes we need to separate from someone or something we hold dear; choices are made and we walk forever after on a different path. In the end we achieve the *conunctio*— the union of opposites, light and dark, male and female, and all opposing subpersonalities; one medieval image depicts this as the Marriage of Fire and Water. We become whole, unified, while remaining aware of our inner polarities. This is the fruit of a lifetime of consciousness.

Earlier, I defined astrology as the formative use of will guided by planetary symbolism for the purpose of unfolding our evolutionary potentials. The focused expression of will enables us to transform life situations, guided by celestial symbolism. Astrology becomes a transformative alchemical discipline as we actively strive to learn from each situation, including stressful transits or progressions. The essence of astrological alchemy is learning to use whatever planetary symbols we are presented with as a catalyst for growth and change. This book has noted many examples of people transforming life situations in the light of planetary symbolism. Here I will share one more of my personal experiences.

Some years ago I was having a very slow period in my psychotherapy practice. I'd had a series of Neptune transits that felt like a dissolving of my practice, a number of clients completed their work with me, my schedule was fairly open and empty, and I felt like I was falling apart. My identity as a psychologist was in a shambles and my self-esteem was at its lowest point ever. I noted that solar arc Saturn was approaching conjunction with my natal Moon. I have Cancer on the Midheaven, so Moon rules my 10th house of career. (Cancer and the Moon rule counseling, providing emotional support to others.) At first I had one of those typical cringing-in-fear reactions, as if this contact inevitably pointed to depression, misery, and failure in my career. Then I practiced the astrological meditation I am describing in this book. I asked, "What is the intention of solar arc Saturn conjunct Moon? What does it *ask* of me?" The answer came from within quite clearly. It meant that I needed to take my work more seriously. I needed to focus on my development as a therapist. I needed to go back into training, to become more committed to my profession. And that is exactly what I did. I joined a training group, making a year's commitment. Within weeks of this decision my practice began to fill up. When we cooperate with our planetary instructions, our lives are alchemically transformed, step by step.

We know whether or not astrology is working from examining the quality of our lives. It may not necessarily mean we become rich or famous or are successful in all our endeavors. But what marks the astrologically conscious life is the capacity to find *meaning* in all events, to always know the deeper significance of what is occurring in our lives. While transiting Pluto was square her natal Pluto on the Ascendant, a woman named Tina's house was burglarized and she lost everything, including every piece of jewelry she owned (Chart #40). Pluto seemed to strip from her many vestiges of her past. Yet that same week her boyfriend gave her an engagement ring. She was able to view the theft as a ritual fleecing, an initiatory stripping away of non-essentials in preparation for receiving the precious ring of love. She remained peaceful and relatively unaffected by her material losses.

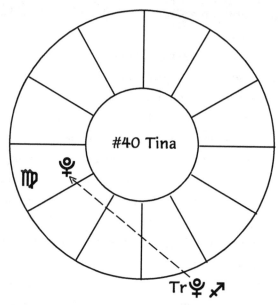

Detachment and Commitment

Tina's story illustrates that the study of astrology teaches us detachment, openness, the willingness to meet whatever comes. We develop evenmindedness. Seen through the lens of planetary symbols, we understand what's happening to us, and we become more fearless because we sense what is supposed to be happening at a given time. Astrology also instructs us to remain committed to living the truth of our being, even if it means taking an unconventional step, even if it means we have less money, or less social status. We stay on our path of creativity, of spiritual awakening, of living simply, or our path of adventure, entrepreneurial risk-taking. We dedicate time to doing the things we love. We follow our path with trust that if we listen to our heart and follow its dictate we will become whole, we will be blessed by the cosmos, we will unfold as we are meant to be. Chakrapani used to counsel me to pursue my interests in yoga, meditation, astrology, spirituality, and writing even though I was making very little money and was not visibly advancing in my career. He advised me to remain in alignment with my *dharma*, the truth of my being, no matter what may come.

Lessons of Love

As noted in Chapter 2, reflection on the birth chart and transits can help us evolve and expand our capacity to love. We begin to express the full spectrum of love, including Venus-Moon tender nurturing, Venus-Mars passionate, sexual love, Venus-Saturn's committed, stable love; and the selfless, devotional love of Venus-Neptune. We also learn an intelligence about life and the cycles of time that help us navigate changing seasons of human relationships, with grace and intelligence. We strive to make our relationships work better by following our transits and progressions, understanding our own personalities, our changing moods and preoccupations; and by studying the chart of our partner/lover/spouse, trying to understand that person's life path and current developmental challenges.

Astrologers often fall into the trap of believing we know exactly what we are looking for in relationships; we have an image of the perfect mate and then expect the other person to embody that image. We look for a compatible Sun or Moon sign, or desirable aspect of Venus, or a strong, grounded Saturn person. If we meet someone with that personal trait and planetary placement we're looking for then we think we're home free. But we have to live with the totality of other people, not just the desirable sides of them to which we are initially attracted. Maybe the person we are drawn into relationship with also has some karmic family complication—for example, the natal Saturn-Pluto conjunction in the 4th house (family) that brings the intrusive, controlling in-laws from hell into your life. One man married a woman with Neptune in her third house; she has two alcoholic brothers, both of whom are insufferable mooches!

A man named Sal fell in love with Nancy, whose Scorpio Sun conjunct Venus seemed really sexy and appealing to him (Chart #41). With a Moon-Neptune conjunction on the Midheaven, Nancy was a very sweet, gentle person. But Nancy also had Mars, Saturn, and Pluto in Leo in the 8th house square the Sun. At the beginning of their relationship Sal had no idea what intense feelings and anger she had inside her, stemming from traumatic events earlier in her life. These events were elucidated by tracing the phases of Nancy's Saturn cycle. At the age of 7, during the time that transiting Saturn was conjunct her Scorpio Sun, Nancy was verbally and sexually abused by her father. From age 14–15 (when transiting Saturn squared her Sun

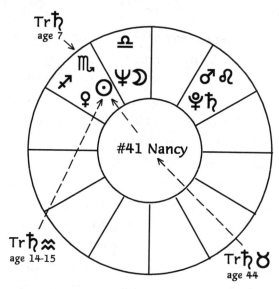

and opposed natal Mars-Saturn-Pluto), she felt that men were constantly making unwanted sexual advances, objectifying her, mistreating her. This infuriated Nancy and she had several acrimonious breakups during her high school years. As an adult, she had a history of abusive relationships with cruel, vindictive men, and several of these partnerships ended in violence. Understandably, she had developed a lot of anger toward men.

At first Nancy was very passionate with Sal. But then things got more complicated. If he said the wrong thing or touched her in the wrong way she was totally traumatized, withdrawing in tears or becoming enraged. Her demeanor would change, and a tough, mean, vicious streak would emerge in her (Scorpio Sun square Mars-Saturn-Pluto in the 8th house). At such times she would become so overbearing and hostile that mild-mannered Sal wanted to hit her on several occasions. Fortunately, he restrained these impulses. Astrology helped Sal understand how he had become a player in Nancy's internal drama. He had become the persecuting, injurious figure Nancy had met so many times in the past, a figure whom she hated and feared. Tracing her life history in the light of her chart symbolism, Sal could see how he too was being cast into the role symbolized by her Mars-Saturn-Pluto square Sun in Scorpio. He could understand the self-protective barriers and the eruptive fury that were written in her cells. He could see Nancy's need to defend herself against the possibility of further attack and injury. At this time, transiting Saturn was in Taurus, opposite her Sun, squaring Mars-Saturn-

Pluto. Clearly her early conflicts with men and her issues around sex and trauma were being reactivated by their relationship, and this was causing some projection and distorted perceptions on her part. But Sal had his part to play in this situation, too. He realized that he had a lot of suppressed anger at women that was being expressed toward Nancy in unconscious ways; he had transiting Pluto square natal Mars at the time. During this period, Sal and Nancy continued to work through highly charged emotional material and grew closer and more deeply intimate with one another. This example illustrates how reflection on the birth charts of our loved ones can help us deepen the quality of our emotional relationships.

In relationships life becomes twice as complicated because we need to understand the complexities of the other person's planetary script, as well as our own. It is as if we now vicariously experience the unfolding of a second chart, which now becomes a part of us. George was living with Abby, who had Moon in Pisces in the 8th house. She had a strong need to share everything, to have no boundaries (Pisces) between their possessions, to wear each other's clothes, to use each other's hair brushes, to have a joint bank account. At first George was quite resistant. He preferred to have his own bank account, his own brush, his own socks. He didn't want to share; it wasn't important to him. But as he came to see understand how Abby's Pisces Moon in the 8th house represented her need to merge possessions and resources, he saw that, as long as he lived with her, sharing was going to be a part of his life. He adapted to her needs; he accepted the symbolism of her chart as something he could learn from. After several years of discussion and disagreement they finally got their shared bank account. Abby was much happier, and that pleased George, too. Embracing the birth chart and inner needs of our loved ones, without violating our own nature, can be an important doorway to wholeness.

Astrology can aid relationship partners in seeing things from the other person's perspective. It can help us articulate to a partner who we are and how we feel. A woman named Terri had Sun, Moon, and Jupiter in Taurus in the 1st house, opposite Neptune in the 7th (Chart #42). She said that love and financial stability were the most important things in her life. Her long-time boyfriend, James, had Sun, Venus, and Neptune conjunct in Scorpio in the 4th house, square Saturn in the 7th house (Chart #43). While Terri

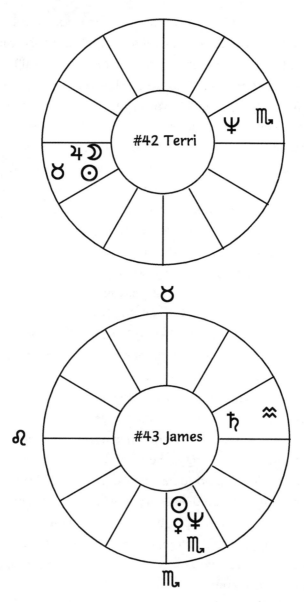

went out to work each day, James stayed home watching movies, smoking dope, and playing the guitar. During a session in which I saw them together, Terri told me that James was a great musician and visionary, and that she supported him in his work because she believed in his dream of musical success. But she was confused about whether she was being a fool, as several of her friends had commented. From one perspective, Terri was naive, blinded by idealism and romantic illusions. But from another perspective, she was exhibiting a strong degree of selfless dedication to James and his potentials (note her Venus-Neptune opposition). Irregardless, Terri now found herself in a crisis. She was feeling increasingly resentful of James's passive dependency and lack of motivation to find a job and support himself—even if in some way his behavior seemed resonant with his birth chart symbolism, not to mention her own Neptune in the 7th house of love and partnership. Indeed, James knew some astrology, and he placed great emphasis on the great destiny he felt was indicated by his birth chart. He pointed out to me that Venus, ruler of his Taurus Midheaven, was conjunct his Sun, ruler of the Leo Ascendant. He felt certain he was going to be a creative force in the music business. I pointed out to him that he also had Sun-Venus-Neptune square to Saturn, and that he had responsibilities to another person (Saturn in the 7th house). He was fortunate to have a partner who was very supportive of his aspirations, but perhaps he needed to be more serious and disciplined about what he was doing, especially if he wanted this relationship to survive.

Terri admitted that she had been seriously considering breaking up with James because he was so irresponsible. She adored him, she said, but he was so impractical and immature. In resonance with the fact that transiting Saturn was currently in Taurus, she now realized that she could not achieve her life's goals on her own, without a partner's financial support. Terri wanted James to fulfill the highest potentials of his birth chart—not only artistic inspiration, but also loving devotion to home and family, and ability to support a household (Sun-Venus-Neptune in the 4th house, square Saturn). Together, Terri and I invited James to embrace and actualize this potential. I also told James that I felt he would grow toward wholeness if he could embrace Terri's chart and its potentials as a part of his own life path. Terri demonstrated compassionate understanding of the challenges James was facing in the world. She was trying to visualize him fulfilling the artistic and spiritual promise of his natal chart. And she was willing to give him time to find himself and figure out what to do with his life. But her patience was wearing thin!

I asked James to imagine what it would be like to have Terri's chart with Sun, Moon, and Jupiter in Taurus. We interpreted her chart symbols together, and James was able to acknowledge the great importance Terri would place on material comfort and financial security. He understood her wish that he find employment and contribute to the household income. He could see how uncomfortable it would make her to have a financially insolvent partner. He was also able to really appreciate the depth of her love and devotion toward him—her Venus opposite Neptune in the 7th house. At the end of our session he made a pact with Terri that he would focus more on the Saturn tasks of work, responsibility, and a mature approach to his professional objectives. A year later, at the time of the Jupiter-Saturn conjunction in Taurus in his 10th house, he found a job, auditioned to play in several nightclubs, and actually got a few gigs. He also borrowed the money to buy recording equipment and began working more seriously on developing his songs. Two years after our initial consultation, they reported to me that James is now working with two other musicians on a recording project, and that they have given several live performances that received favorable reviews. Recently he was asked to contribute to a film soundtrack. He is achieving his dreams, reaching his goals. Transiting Saturn is now entering James' 11th house, so he is getting involved with a group, and his increased income has satisfied Terri, who (with transiting Saturn now in her 2nd house) is carefully saving their money for a down payment to buy a house.

A lesbian couple, Julie and Vicky, came to consult with me because they had been fighting a lot and wanted to understand the dynamics of their relationship (charts #44 and 45). They had considered breaking up, but they owned a house together and their lives were deeply entwined, so a breakup was not a casual matter. I noted some situational factors that seemed to symbolize their current discord: Julie had transiting Mars retrograde in Sagittarius square her natal Mars in Pisces for a six month period, and progressed Sun quincunx Mars. Vicky had progressed Mars quincunx Sun; solar arc Mars square Pluto; solar arc Pluto conjunct her 4th house cusp; also, her progressed Moon was in Aries in the 10th house. I could see a lot of symbolism that denoted willfulness and conflict, but what could I say in one astrological consultation that would help them work through these dynamics? Couples work with astrology is a fine art and a tricky business. I have no formula for success other than to follow the lead of my intuition and to strive for a voicing of both people's viewpoints. In this instance, I felt the pressure of their hope, and expectation, that this session would be a catalytic event enabling them move through their uncomfortable impasse.

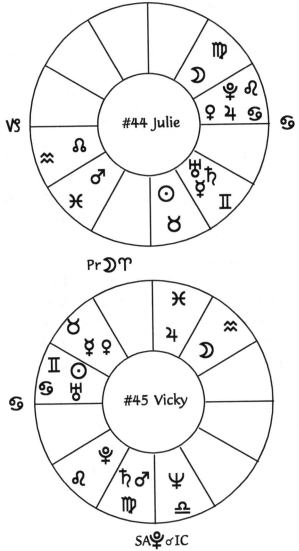

I noted that Vicky's Mars and Saturn in Virgo were conjunct Julie's Moon in Virgo. Julie felt that Vicky constantly criticized her; this was deeply wounding to Julie, evoking memories of how her own mother had berated her (Virgo Moon). This, in turn made Julie feel anxious, contracted, and unloved. For her part, Vicky felt that her accurate, discerning perceptions were always discounted by Julie, and that she wasn't allowed to have a voice in the relationship; she was tired of suppressing her feelings and her opinions. Viewing this pattern in the light of her Mars-Saturn in Virgo in the 3rd house, square her Sun in the 12th house, Vicky was able to identify a core wound around her father and older brothers, with whom she had always argued bitterly. She always felt unseen by these men, and she felt unseen now (12th house Sun). Vicky's Mars and Saturn opposed Julie's Mars in Pisces; Vicky felt that Julie avoided conflict, and said, "Whenever I get angry or assertive you just fall apart." We explored how Julie responded to conflict by withdrawal and retreat into feelings of desolate loneliness. Julie said, "When you are angry at me I feel like I can't reach you, I can't get any love, so I go away." All of this was aptly described by Mars in Pisces. Also, Vicky's Uranus was conjunct Julie's Venus in Cancer, triggering in Julie a touchiness and aloofness, a way of breaking contact abruptly.

Vicky had Moon in Aquarius directly opposite Pluto. She admitted that at times she was extremely controlling, just like her own mother. With solar arc Pluto conjunct her IC, many of Vicky's most deeply buried family conflicts and resentments were being reawakened, and she felt a fire of anger burning within her. I told her that this was a crucial time to discharge her deep rage about her family and to find more positive expressions of her forceful personality. With progressed Moon in Aries in her 10th house, self-assertiveness was fully appropriate, as long as she realized she wasn't always going to get her way. And, with Mars-Saturn in Virgo, Vicky knew she could indeed be extremely critical and perfectionistic, just like her father. Both women could now see how this relationship offered the opportunity to heal emotions and interactional patterns stemming from their early parent-child relationships, so they could meet each other from the heart once again.

I also wanted Vicky and Julie to know that there was much that connected them astrologically in a positive way. Julie's Sun is conjunct Vicky's Mercury; they have many interests in common, stimulate each other's minds, and have excellent communication when they are not fighting! Julie's Saturn is conjunct Vicky's Sun in the 12th house, symbolizing the responsibilities (Saturn) they share, as well as their ongoing serious conversation about dreams, symbols, the inner life of the Spirit (12th house). Vicky's Venus sextiles Julie's Mars, indicating physical attraction and mutual desire. Vicky's Moon is conjunct Julie's north node, showing strong emotional affinity; and Vicky's Venus in Taurus is conjunct Julie's IC—symbol of the beautiful home they share and their basic compatibility as domestic partners. They have Venus sextile Venus, showing compatible tastes, affection, and happiness in each other's company, which unites them as lovers despite the discordant dynamics that sometimes threaten to tear them apart. Vicky's Venus sextiles Julie's Saturn, showing the longevity and commitment of their relationship. These last examples demonstrate that another contribution astrology makes to our lives is its ability to help us live together, love one another more deeply, and walk together in peace.

A Final Meditation

Go inside to the deepest place of inner silence and tranquility you can reach. With the Buddha's infinite compassion witness the entire wheel of time and manifestation arising and unfolding according to steady cyclic rhythms. Cycles within cycles begin, culminate, decay, end, and begin again. You have experienced all pleasures, all sorrows. You have been all life forms, all twelve creatures and phases of the zodiac. You encompass all planets, all signs, all evolutionary conditions, within the circumference of your consciousness.

Now meditate on your own birthmap and your current transits and progressions. From this place of serenity ask, "What is the secret purpose of this natal planetary placement, this aspect, this transit or progression? What does the universe intend from this? What am I supposed to learn? What steps am I asked to take in order to cooperate with the divine intention?" Consider what your chart wants to convey to you. Visualize an outcome that is in alignment with the planetary symbols, and that resonates in your being as a positive evolutionary step. Visualize yourself committing to actions that will help you reach your goals. Use astrology as an active and creative process to manifest your own vision for your life.

When you feel complete, spend a few minutes writing down some thoughts in your journal.

The study of astrology is a training course that takes a lifetime to complete. It is an intensive instruction in a life of consciousness. The spiritual lessons of astrology instill in us the qualities of discernment, tranquility, wisdom, detachment from transitory appearances (this too shall pass); and ability to discern the cosmic intelligence at work behind all events—the divine intention. As we visualize the most evolved expression of each planet, each transit and progression, astrology becomes an alchemical key to our personal transformation.

The benefits we receive from the study of astrology are immense. The birth chart reveals guiding images of our potentials, which we strive to actualize through our focused use of will. We gain the power of forethought and planning for future probabilities. We meet the immense demands life makes on us by accepting the constant form-building and form-sustaining tests and disciplines of Saturn. We live in harmony within cycles, from planting to harvest, through decay and dormancy, to spring rebirth.

Astrology is an empowering mystical-instructional method, for it teaches us to rely on our own judgement, our own understanding of planetary symbols. Our authority of interpretation comes from inside us, not from reading medieval texts or the pronouncements of ancient sages and *rishis* (seers). In the practice of astrology and meditation, *we* are the rishis, the clear-seeing ones. In the sacred moment of spontaneously revealed truth, we tap into the power of focused translucency through which astrology pours its knowledge and insight into our receptive minds.

We are fortunate indeed to be guided through our lives by astrology. May our study and celebration of time and its phases assist us in reaching our highest evolutionary goals. May the light of wisdom reveal itself to each of us through the practice of this sacred art, and may we hold this knowledge with gratitude and reverence.

Swaha

Obeisance to the Lords of Time

Appendices

APPENDIX A

The Twelve Yogas of the Zodiac

The twelve signs of the zodiac represent twelve phases of evolution that repeat eternally. Enlightenment means to participate fully and consciously in each of these phases of existence. They are *yogas* or life roads, paths to the center, facets of our wholeness.

In the beginning is **Pisces**, the ocean, the unmanifest, formless Being-Consciousness-Bliss, which precedes creation and all visible form. It is the realm of dreams, possibilities, karmic seeds, and archetypes that provide the raw material out of which our lives unfold.

Aries represents emergent individuality, focus on the individual ego identity, and assertion of the will. It is vitality, autonomy, and intention. Aries represents Hercules and his might, the insistent forward movement of the Ram, the hero archetype, seeking one's individual aims with intensity and dynamic intention. This is the phase where the personal will becomes operative. Later we will strive to align our individual will and efforts with a collective will, the need of a greater Whole. Aries symbolizes desire and exuberance, activation of *prana*, the vital force—emerging as instinctual drives or as spontaneous action impelled by a spiritual need.

Taurus represents our evolving connection to the physical world. It is the evolutionary phase of grounding, calm sensate awareness of the physical body and the physical world, and growth through the experiences of acquisition and ownership. Taurus is the yoga of money, financial stability, comfort, and sensual enjoyment. It is the practice of *karma yoga*, the yoga of action and its harvest. With awareness of the law of karma—cause and effect—we plant the seeds of good actions. The intrinsic value and practical usefulness of our activities lead to positive energy exchange with the world. Taurus is the Cow and the Bull, the fertility of nature, our relationship to the Earth.

Gemini represents the evolution of speech, language, and communication. It is the phase of thinking, learning, and pursuit of facts and knowledge, and mobility to explore the environment. It represents perception, information processing, evolving an informed intellect, and communicating the story of one's human experience. Gemini is what the yogis call *manas*, the lower mind, the outward movement of awareness into realms of endless multiplicity. It is also the path of consciousness through right speech and right thought; and through *mantra yoga*—where resonant sound stills the mind and attunes us to Source, the original sound, the original vibration of creation. Gemini is Hermes, the divine Messenger, the scribe of the Emerald Tablet, the sacred word.

Cancer is the phase of personal orientation, in which we seek security and a sense of place within the emotional fortress provided by home, family and close emotional attachments to others. Cancer is the path of feeling, caring deeply about others, and creating a nurturing, comforting physical and emotional environment in our home and family. I sometimes call Cancer the phase of *mama yoga*, the path of developing a more caring, nurturing, feelingful response to the world. It is the path of the Mother, our experience of giving and receiving the deepest sustaining love and nurturance. Cancer is the Crab and the Turtle, symbols of sensitivity, movement into a protective inner shell.

Leo is the evolutionary phase in which the individual ego gains the power of self-expression and of externalizing personal identity. We express our inner light and joy through play, dance, performance, playfulness, and through being the conduit for children and their light to come into the world. Leo is the way of the performer, the path of self-expression, creativity, and joy. With maturation, any arrogant sense of greatness, specialness, or entitlement is tempered as we begin to express our individuality with humility and heart. Leo is *ananda*, joy and solar splendor, the King and Queen archetypes, the radiance of the royal self.

Virgo is the evolutionary phase of self-reflection and self-improvement, and the quest for purity and health. It is the path of examining ourselves, making necessary changes in our habits, improving our skills, and learning to do our jobs better. Virgo is also the yoga of work, training, apprenticeship and discipleship, following a spiritual discipline. Virgo represents the practice of constancy in mindfulness, conscious labor as service to life. It is *viveka*, discriminating wisdom, Manjushri Buddha, the power to cut through neurosis with clear, discerning awareness. Virgo is the Worker, the Disciple. We manifest here a disciplined commitment to service and self-betterment.

Libra is the evolutionary phase of evolution through friendship, relationship, and cooperation with others. It is the phase of attraction, coupling, interpersonal harmony, cooperation, and accommodating to another person's needs. It is the path of the Lover and the Beloved, the couple's journey, the path of love, *bhakti yoga*—devotional heart yoga. We see in the face of our beloved a pure beauty and pure love that is a reflection of our own true nature. Libra is the sign of Aphrodite, Romeo and Juliet, John and Yoko, and all persons who attain wholeness through the path of marriage.

Scorpio is the evolutionary phase of interpersonal fusion or interpersonal crisis. It is the path of learning to merge our assets, our intention, our very being, with another person. Scorpio represents the dynamic transmission of energy or resources from one person to another, investment, funds received from others through gifts, inheritance, credit and loans. It is sexual union, or the strife that creates angry separation of lovers. Scorpio symbolizes the interpersonal conflicts and power struggles we must resolve to achieve a condition of unified intention. In this phase, we become involved in a network of agreements with other individuals or institutions, which are trusts we must honor. The result of our interpersonal commitments is emotional intimacy, financial gains, spiritual empowerment, the awakening of the inner fire. Scorpio is encounter with Shadow, Kali Ma, ordeals of death-rebirth. It is Snake, Eagle, Phoenix, Quetzalcoatl—the plumed serpent. Scorpio is the rousing of the ascending current of the *kundalini shakti*. We awaken our dormant evolutionary powers.

Sagittarius is the evolutionary phase of adventure, education, intellectual inquiry, defining theories and concepts, and adherence to moral codes or philosophical doctrines. Sagittarius is the path of acquiring true knowledge through travel and education, the company of the wise, and through a life of study and reflection. Sagittarius also signifies hope, anticipation, optimism, planning for the future. It is the phase of striving for advancement and progress, to bring our ideals to life. Sagittarius governs our search for truth and meaning, and active consecration to our ideals. It represents the path of *jnana yoga*, the path of knowledge. Its archetypes include Priest, Teacher, Centaur, and the goddess Artemis.

Capricorn is the evolutionary phase of ambition, accomplishment, and incarnation of our archetypal potentials. It is the path of serving the whole through masterful performance of one's role and achievement of one's goals through sustained efforts, and through skillfulness in managing the many facets of one's life. Capricorn represents the accomplished self, fully realized ego identity. It is the yoga of fulfilling our *dharma*, our life task, our truth of being. Its central concern is authority and responsibility, social position, the exercise of one's powers within an organized social framework. Capricorn is Time, Father, Senex (Wise Old Man or Woman). It is the path of mastery through accomplishment.

Aquarius is the evolutionary phase of social awareness and group consciousness. It is the path of surfing the wave of collective change, joining others who share common goals and ideals, through involvement in politics, social activism, or any group activity. Aquarius is the phase in which we seek the *sangha*, the community of spiritual friends and allies, who share common visions, ideals, and goals for the future. It is the phase of gathering together, participation in social change and all collective movements. It represents freedom from dominant social norms and traditions, and expression of the spirit of innovation. Its central concerns are futurity, equality, and originality. Aquarius is the Trickster, Heyoka (sacred clown), Revolutionary, the Post-Revolutionary Society. Aquarius is the archetype of perfected Man, the destiny of humankind, the future social and planetary condition of wholeness, balance, equality, and unity-in-diversity at the consummation of human history.

Pisces is the evolutionary phase of return to our original condition of infinite light and consciousness. It is the path of merging into Spirit, surrendering, offering self in service, resting in the still point at the center. It is the experience of ego-transcendence, spiritual awakening, union with the divine. It symbolizes dreaming, envisioning, imagining, yielding to the divine will. It is the phase of generosity, spirituality, nonduality. Pisces represents the Fish flowing in stillness, at one with the water. It is the path of *moksha*, liberation in the formless sea of Spirit. Pisces represents the inward movement of awareness, consciousness merging back into Source.

Ultimately we become all signs, all moments, all phases of evolution. We develop what Dane Rudhyar calls the *mind of wholeness*, a consciousness that encompasses all phases in their totality.

APPENDIX B

Understanding the Jupiter-Saturn Cycle

Each system of astrology is built around certain core principles. Vedic astrology is built on the system of planetary strengths and weaknesses, planetary *yogas* and *dasa/bhukti* periods. Medieval European and Islamic astrology emphasized essential dignities and debilities, nocturnal versus diurnal birthtimes, house lords, and planetary parts. Some modern systems of chart interpretation focus on the influence of midpoints and harmonics. And the foundation of the humanistic-transpersonal astrology pioneered by Dane Rudhyar is the understanding of cycles in human experience—the awareness that everything has a beginning, a formative period, a culmination or climactic moment, reevaluation and growth of consciousness, often accompanied by the breakdown of structures; and finally a moment of expectancy in preparation for a new cycle of growth that is about to begin.

Most of us are aware of the Sun-Moon cycle, the most basic cycle of the evolving life force. We all know the importance of watching the phases of the Moon each month, and we can use this cycle to time the rhythms of our basic life activities. There is a New Moon, waxing crescent Moon (first quarter), Full Moon, waning crescent (third quarter), and the balsamic Moon at the end of the cycle. We can apply the same cyclic principles in studying other interplanetary relationships. To do so, we distinguish between *cycles of planetary position*—for example the Saturn cycle, Saturn's transiting relationship to its own natal position—and *cycles of interplanetary relationship*, defined by the cyclic interaction between any two planets (for example, the monthly interplay between the Sun and Moon).

Here I will explore one of the most important interplanetary cycles, the cycle of Jupiter and Saturn. In ancient times the cycle of these two planets were used to predict collective events of great importance, events affecting kings and kingdoms. It has a long history of usage in the astrological tradition. In the book, *Mundane Astrology*, Charles Harvey writes,

> These two planets used to be known as the "Great Chronocrators," or rulers of the ages. Their cycle can be considered the ground base of human development which marks the interaction between the perception of ideas, potentialities, possibilities (Jupiter) and their manifestation in the concrete material world (Saturn).[70]

Jupiter and Saturn as a planetary pair symbolize the urge to find a mode of meaningful participation in social living. Alexander Ruperti called Jupiter and Saturn the planets of social destiny.[71] They are concerned with the formation of our sense of social purpose and direction, our quest for concrete achievements in the world. They are the planets most concerned with vocational development, the development of our occupation and our pursuit of success. They are the planets of positive, constructive social activity. The ongoing relationship between these two planets marks major phases of our developing life's work, and the conjunction in particular is a time when we can form a new sense of social purpose or direction.

The twenty year cycle of Jupiter and Saturn defines the story of our efforts to make something of ourselves and our lives in this world. Jupiter-Saturn as a pair represent a positive, focused attitude, the attempt to define and focus our ambitions, what we seek to achieve. They signify our search for success in all of our activities. The major phases of their cycle correspond to turning points in our efforts to actualize our ambitions.

At the time of Jupiter-Saturn conjunctions we start to see new directions for our ambitions. We begin to formulate new goals for social activity and achievement. If the transiting conjunction (or other major phases of the cycle) falls in a powerful place in our natal chart, we may see specific accomplishments occurring at that time. The conjunction is the beginning of a formative process that will continue to unfold over the next twenty years.

Looking Back at the Past Cycle

Before we look forward at how the recent Jupiter-Saturn conjunction in Taurus may influence us, it is helpful look back at the cycle that has recently ended. The previous Jupiter-Saturn conjunction formed between November 1980 and August 1981, in the first ten degrees of Libra. Look at your own chart and find where that conjunction fell. At the time of the Jupiter-Saturn conjunction we make commitments to major projects. Because the last conjunction fell in Libra, love and relationships of all kinds (not only romantic or marital ones) were central to our new life-direction. One woman who had the conjunction in her 5th house decided to get married specifically for the purpose of having children. This was the formative commitment of the conjunction. Whatever is set in motion at the conjunction is carried forward and has continuing ramifications over the next twenty years, according to the sign and natal house the conjunction falls in, and the aspects formed to natal planets.

A woman who had Jupiter-Saturn conjunct her natal Mercury-Jupiter applied to college and decided she wanted to write an illustrated children's story. Another woman, with the conjunction in her 9th house met her spiritual teacher (9th house). My own spiritual guide, Swami Muktananda, had a Jupiter-Saturn conjunction conjunct his MC in 1961. Over the next twenty years, this man, who had spent the previous thirty years living as a monk wandering around India and meditating in solitude, suddenly became a famous teacher, a world renowned guru.

A woman with the conjunction in her 2nd house became a banker at the last conjunction. Her life became focused on creating financial stability and wealth. In contrast, a woman with the Jupiter-Saturn conjunction in her 12th house conjunct natal Neptune formed a commitment to a spiritual path at that time. She was also somewhat confused and up in the air about her goals in the external world.

For me, the Libra conjunction also fell in the 12th house, the realm of astrology and metaphysics, spirituality, and mysticism. This was a period in which I was not drawn at all toward a conventional career or social ambitions. I was in total retreat, immersed in dreamwork, meditation, and studies of astrology, symbols, myth and religion. All of this seemed totally impractical, yet my entire being was focused inward in these ways. Then, at the time of the Jupiter-Saturn conjunction, life provided me with a remarkable opportunity. I formed an association with a Venezuelan astrologer, Andrés Takra (I called him "The Wildman of Caracas"), who hired me as his assistant. I got paid to have daily private lessons in astrology! I formed a commitment to the path of mysticism and spiritual study. I became the Wildman's apprentice and formed a new social identity as an astrologer that has continued since 1981. My entire career has been an emanation of the work I did at that time. In addition, the Jupiter-Saturn conjunction squared my natal Mercury in the 3rd house. Takra hired me to ghost-write and edit his book, *The Wisdom of Sidereal Astrology*.[72] This set in motion a period of twenty years in which I would be engaged extensively in writing. This was the inception of a cycle in which my Mercury abilities would come forth. That is when I became a writer: Jupiter-Saturn square Mercury.

At the conjunction a new commitment is formed. We start putting energy into a project. We develop certitude that this is what we are going to do with our lives, and that this is what we hope to achieve. At the opening Jupiter-Saturn square we are asked to take some decisive step toward actualizing the purpose and commitment formed at the conjunction. A woman named Brenda had the 1981 Jupiter-Saturn conjunction conjunct her natal Venus-Neptune in Libra. She began to teach art (Libra rules art and beauty). Jupiter-Saturn were transiting her 11th house, so her teaching involved not just lecturing but also facilitating group process (11th house). In the spring of 1986, Jupiter was in Pisces square Saturn in Sagittarius. At this time, Brenda expanded her school and went national with her work through promotional advertising and a lecture tour. With transiting Jupiter passing through her 4th house, she established a new base of operations, moving to a major city and opening two new centers. Natal Saturn was in Brenda's 9th house, so note that the whole cycle referred to her innate desire and capacity to teach.

The opening square of any cycle is a time for decisive action to make the dream or ambition become real, to make it happen, to fulfill the purpose of the cycle, the purpose that was revealed at the conjunction. In 1986 I made the decision that to be an effective astrologer in this culture I needed psychological training and technique. Thus, I returned to school to become a psychotherapist. Transiting Saturn was in my 3rd house in Sagittarius (education), while Jupiter in Pisces passed through my 6th house—the house of vocational planning, training, and skill enhancement.

Ideally we should see some climactic outcome by the time of the Jupiter-

Saturn opposition. The opposition phase of the last Jupiter-Saturn cycle lasted a long time, from 1989–1991 (Sept–Nov 1989, 7–11° Cancer/ Capricorn; July 1990, 23°Cancer/Capricorn; and March–May 1991, 4–7° Leo/ Aquarius). A woman who had Jupiter conjunct her MC and Saturn at her IC received a large donation from a millionaire philanthropist, which enabled her to expand her business. A man with Saturn conjunct MC and Jupiter conjunct IC in 1989 entered a period of notable accomplishment in his legal career, arguing two cases before the State Supreme Court. Another man, with Jupiter conjunct MC and Saturn conjunct IC, found a publisher for his novel after years of work to complete it.

At the Jupiter-Saturn opposition Brenda wrote a series of instructional videos based on the work she started at the conjunction and expanded at the opening square. Transiting Saturn was in her 3rd house (writing) opposite transiting Jupiter was in her 9th house; these videos described her complete philosophy of art, education, and creativity. It was the culmination of years of work.

The third quarter square of Jupiter-Saturn occurred in February 1995 at 13° Sag/Pisces and in November 1995, at 19° Sag/Pisces. The closing square of any cycle is a time of reorientation of attitude and commitment. There is often the beginning of a breakdown of form, because your attitude is changing. Brenda lost interest in her business at the closing square and thought about selling the company. The closing square is the beginning of the end of our commitment to the project that has defined that cycle. One woman told me that at the closing square she was burdened by a sense of a failure, feeling that he had not achieved the goals she set for herself at the conjunction. I reminded her of a key astrological concept: that there is always another cycle, another opportunity, another chance to fulfill the unfinished evolutionary business of the past.[73] The upcoming Jupiter-Saturn conjunction in the spring of 2000 symbolized, for all of us, the beginning of an entirely new cycle, an opportunity to define new aspirations and goals, and to choose where to focus our energies for constructive activity for the next twenty years.

The Conjunction in Taurus

The Jupiter-Saturn conjunction in May–June 2000 was at 23–24° Taurus. Look at your chart and find where these degrees fall in your chart, the house placement of the conjunction and any aspects formed. This is where your life has started going, where your life is heading, where you need to focus your energies. This is an area where ideally personal commitments have been made, and where you are striving for tangible achievement of your life goals, the goal of the Jupiter-Saturn.

In the study of astrology we learn to use the formative power of the will in alignment with planetary symbolism, for the purpose of evolving and unfolding all of our potentials. Thus, the Jupiter-Saturn conjunction means what we make it mean. It is not a question of "What is going to happen to me at this time?" but rather, "What am I going to make of this transit? How do I choose to invent the meaning of the Jupiter-Saturn conjunction?" That moment has lasting impact on us all. For example, a woman who wanted to buy a house was going to have the conjunction in her 4th house. She lined up her loan from a bank, months ahead of time. She got ready for the conjunction, and by the time it occurred she was ready to proceed, she found the right place, and she purchased (Taurus) home and property (4th house). A new cycle of life began for her.

For all of us, the recent Jupiter-Saturn in Taurus has made financial stability a major issue. The conjunction initiated a time of active striving to earn more money, a time of greater focus on financial commitments and generating wealth. Jupiter and Saturn conjunct in Taurus means taking charge of our financial destiny. Taurus is the sign of the ox, a beast of burden. Pulling a cart like an ox requires strength, determination, persistence. We place greater emphasis on working hard and saving money.

The conjunction in Taurus reminds us that, to counterbalance the electric but airy, disembodied quality of the growing electronic culture (Uranus in Aquarius), we also need to connect to nature, the earth. Connect to the consciousness of the cow. Feel your roundness and solidity, the strength of your legs beneath you, connected through your feet to the earth below. Chew your life experience slowly and thoroughly. Cut through neurotic speed. Be at ease. Log off the internet and hug a tree. Feel your connection to the plant kingdom. Taurus symbolizes the physical world, the biosphere.

Thus, the conjunction asks us to value nature and confront how we've trashed our precious natural resources. Ecological awareness and preservation of the environment become central priorities. Atmospheric degradation and pollution of the biosphere require that we learn new ways to meet our basic survival needs. Taurus corresponds to the level of agrarian societies, learning the arts of cultivation, so this recent conjunction has asked us to cultivate crops and products of concrete value and intrinsic worth, crafted with artistry.

Our attitudes toward money change, becoming more realistic, more resourceful. This may mean a determination to earn more money; or it could mean recognition of the things in life we value besides money, such as time, nature, music, love and friendship. For me, these are the true wealth of my life, the sources of joy; and I find that as I put my energy into these areas of my life, I always have enough money. You may wish to try this for yourself.

The Conjunction Through the Houses

Now, let us consider the general meaning of the conjunction in the twelve houses of the birth chart. These descriptions of general themes are intended to be suggestive, not exhaustive, and of course will be modified by the aspects the Jupiter-Saturn conjunction makes to our natal planets.

House I: Commitment to the project of creating a more stable, viable social identity. New professional demeanor, focus on professional advancement. Greater professionalism in appearance and attitude. New spirit of discipline and seriousness of purpose. Stronger intention to become successful and to gain substance and wealth over time. Decisions to assume a more responsible or adult role in the world, such as that of parent (especially if natal Moon or Saturn are placed in the 1st house).

House II: Commitment to the project of earning money. Setting financial goals. Starting to earn more money. Becoming more focused on getting tangible rewards for one's efforts. Beginning to meet the material problems of existence more effectively. Significant purchases.

House III: Commitment to the project of learning. Learning or education gains a practical focus. Acquiring knowledge that will be of practical value and will help in earning more money. Getting schooling that will directly lead to a good job. Reading financial news, following markets. Learning basic money skills, such as accounting, bookkeeping, money management; reading financial news and trends.

House IV: Commitment to the projects of home and family. Focus on home or property value. Possible purchase of land or home, or expenditures for home/property improvements. Earning money to support family development. Major events affecting family. Opening a place of business.

House V: Commitment to the project of having or raising children. Expenditure on children. Planning for child's education. Milestones in child's social/professional advancement. Greater seriousness about creativity, and investment in creative projects. Seeking profit through speculation or gambling.

House VI: Commitment to the projects of health and self-betterment. Getting better health care or insurance. Seeking or finding a better paying job. Expenditure for health care or health products. Greater commitment to self-improvement, skill enhancement, job training, health program, or spiritual practice. More investment in vocational/occupational role, job responsibilities. Greater responsibility for management of workers, employees.

House VII: Commitment to the project of meaningful relationships with others. Important developments in personal friendships or relationships. Decision to get married. Relationship with ambitious or successful person. Milestones in partner's career choice or advancement. Business partnership forms.

House VIII: Commitment to the project of shared financial ventures. Business investments. Shared financial decisions or undertakings. Important developments, and potential growth, in marital finances. Partner begins to earn more money. Deeper interpersonal fusion, through touch, sexual union. Matters concerning inheritance, financial legacy. Receiving loans from financial institutions and increased involvement in investment strategies. Financial empowerment through deeper interpersonal commitments. New efforts to get out of debt.

House IX: Commitment to the project of cultivating wisdom through travel and study. Paying for education. Study of economic theory, physical sciences, or practical, down-to-earth subjects. Payment for teaching, publication. Professional plans require education. Expenses related to travel, schooling. Profiting from one's knowledge. International business opportunities. Growth through publishing, advertising, self-promotion.

House X: Commitment to the project of success in career. Important career developments. Professional opportunity and progress, expansion. More authority in profession. Greater responsibility, financial reward from career. Reputation grows. External recognition of self-worth.

House XI: Commitment to the project of community, group, or political involvement. Deeper involvement in a group. Organizational commitments. Increased political consciousness, activism. Fund-raising for an organization or political cause.

House XII: Commitment to the project of enlightenment, self-transcendence, consciousness expansion. Pursuing the inner journey. Discovery of the mysteries of life. New understanding of astrology and the laws of karma. Formation of goals and ambitions focused around spiritual goals and values. Assuming the social identity of a mystic, committed meditator, astrologer, monk/nun, philanthropist, or servant of humanity.

Now map out where the subsequent phases of the current Jupiter-Saturn cycle occur in your chart. Examine each phase of the cycle and envision how the cycle may unfold for you. Imagine the possibilities.

Jupiter-Saturn conjunction, 24 Taurus, June 2000

Jupiter 11 Scorpio square Saturn 11 Leo, December 2005

Jupiter 28 Pisces opposite Saturn 28 Virgo, May 2010, just as Uranus enters Aries

Jupiter 3 Aries opposite Saturn 3 Libra, August 2010

Jupiter 15 Aries opposite Saturn 15 Libra, March 2011

Jupiter 29 Leo square Saturn 29 Scorpio, August 2015

Jupiter 17 Virgo square Saturn, 17 Sagittarius, March 2016

Jupiter stationary direct, 14 Virgo square Saturn retrograde
14 Sagittarius, May 2016

Jupiter-Saturn conjunction 1 Aquarius, December 2020

Attunement to the Jupiter-Saturn cycle can help us walk a path of steady growth, focused commitments, and gradual achievement of our goals.

Footnotes

Introduction

1. D. Rudhyar, *An Astrological Mandala* (New York: Vintage, 1973) , p. 385.

Chapter 1

2. D. Rudhyar, *The Practice of Astrology as a Technique in Human Understanding* (New York: Penguin Books, 1968), pp. 29, 37.

3. See G. Bogart, *Astrology and Spiritual Awakening* (Berkeley, CA: Dawn Mountain Press, 1994), pp. 75—7.

4. D. Rudhyar, *An Astrological Mandala* (New York: Vintage, 1973), p. 308.

5. Grant Lewi was born June 8, 1902, at 8:35 am EST, in Albany, New York. He died on July 15, 1951 in Tucson, Arizona, time unknown. Apparently Lewi predicted the exact date of his death. Lewi had natal Sun conjunct Pluto in Gemini, so he may have had a longstanding interest in understanding his death. Transiting Saturn was in Virgo and it had been square natal Sun-Pluto for the previous year; he may have noticed some signs or symptoms of poor health. Transiting Saturn closely trined natal Saturn in the 6th house of health. I have no conclusive evidence of how Lewi was able to make this prediction so precisely, to the day. What I have been able to determine, with the help of David Kesten, is as follows: On the date of his death, Lewi's progressed Ascendant at 17 Virgo 51, squared his natal Pluto at 18 Gemini 08. His progressed Sun at 3 Leo 39 was semisquare Pluto, with an orb of 31min or about six months; this measurement is not precise enough for an exact prediction, but it is still significant. Also, in September, 1950 there was a solar eclipse in Virgo that closely squared his natal Sun-Pluto. On the date of death, transiting Saturn was at 27 Virgo 23, *exactly* conjunct Lewi's solar arc Ascendant at 27 Virgo 23. The

transiting north node of the Moon, at 12 Pisces 26 was semisquare natal Saturn at 27 Capricorn 02. And Lewi's solar arc Pluto at 4 Leo 59 closely squared natal Venus at 5 Taurus 08, ruler of his Libra 4th house cusp, and thus the planet associated with the end of life. His progressed Moon at 26 Aries 36, was conjunct his MC at 27 Aries 59. Aries rules the head; Lewi died suddenly from a cerebral hemorrhage.

6. D. Rudhyar, *An Astrological Triptych* (Santa Fe, NM: Aurora Press), p. 104.

7. C. G. Jung, *Memories, Dreams, Reflections* (New York: Vintage Books) p.196.

Chapter 2

8. See "Finding a Spiritual Path," in G. Bogart, *Astrology and Spiritual Awakening* (Berkeley, CA: Dawn Mountain Press), 1994.

9. See "Astrology and Multi-Level Initiation," in G. Bogart, *Therapeutic Astrology* (Berkeley, CA: Dawn Mountain Press, 1996), pp. 101—7.

10. Lilly wrote this of his own teacher, Evans: "For money he would willingly give contrary judgements." Lilly goes on to say that Evans "was much addicted to debauchery, and then very abusive and quarrelsome, seldom without a black eye, or one mischief or other." *William Lilly's History of His Life and Times* (London: T. Davies, Publisher, 1774), p. 31.

11. J. Holmes, *John Bowlby and Attachment Theory* (New York, Routledge, 1993).

12. Charles Carter says Sun-Mars denotes energy, strength, decisiveness, knowing what one wishes and intends, as well as combativeness, and tendency toward accident or strain through overwork or risk-taking. C. Carter, *The Astrological Aspects* (London: Fowler, 1930).

13. For Sun-Jupiter aspects, Carter notes preference for relaxation and easy living, imprudence, carelessness, blind optimism, being selfish, lazy, and excessive in diet.

14. Carter notes that Sun-Saturn aspects bring patience, success through hard work, constructive, well-considered actions, capacity to govern and shape destinies of communities, or to build up great businesses.

15. D. Rudhyar, *The Sun is Also a Star* (Santa Fe, NM: Aurora Press, 1975).

16. The 5th house is traditionally said to govern gambling and risk-taking.

17. G. Bogart, *Therapeutic Astrology* (Berkeley, CA: Dawn Mountain Press, 1996), pp. 163.

18. R. Ebertin, *The Combination of Stellar Influences* (Aalen, Germany: Ebertin-Verlag, 1972), p.128.

19. G. Bogart, *Therapeutic Astrology* (Berkeley, CA: Dawn Mountain Press, 1996), p. 128.

20. In the language of cosmobiology, this pattern would be described as Sun=Mars-Pluto, described by Ebertin as "Injury, accident, violent measures, an upset or shock caused through the intervention of Higher Power." R. Ebertin, *The Combination of Stellar Influences* (Aalen, Germany: EbertinVerlag, 1972), p. 163.

21. See Appendix B. The study of interplanetary transit cycles is explained in Alexander Ruperti's book, *Cycles of Becoming* (Sebastopol, CA: CRCS Publications, 1978).

22. Shelley Jordan told me, "A great Mars-Jupiter example is composer Richard Wagner, who had Mars in Aquarius conjunct his Midheaven, opposite Jupiter in Leo. Wagner wrote gargantuan operas, which were enormous projects that took months or years to produce, and which had strong political and social implications (Mars in Aquarius)."

23. In the medieval literature of alchemy, Mars corresponds to the element *sulphur,* which Jung viewed as a symbol for the active substance in the psyche, the motive factor in consciousness. On the one hand sulphur symbolizes will; on the other hand it symbolizes compulsion, an involuntary motivation or impulse. According to Jungian analyst Edward Edinger,

    Sulphur is desirousness. It is the fire of libido, which is life energy itself. If you frustrate desirousness it turns vicious. It turns demanding. It turns tyrannical, power-ridden. It immediately demonstrates its true nature when it's denied fulfillment. [In Jung's Vision Seminars] he tells us how to deal with desirousness. Jung wrote that, "The fire of desirousness is the element that must be fought against in Brahmanism, In Buddhism, in Tantrism, in Manicheanism, in Christianity. It's also important in psychology ... When you indulge in desirousness ... you give the animus or the anima an object; then it comes out in the world instead of staying inside in its place ... But if you can say, Yes, I desire it and I shall try to get it but I do not have to have it, if I decide to renounce, I can renounce it; then there is no chance for the animus or anima. Otherwise you are governed by your desires, you are possessed ... But if you have put your animus or anima into a bottle you are free of possession, even though you may be having a bad time inside, because when your devil has a bad time you have a bad time ... Of course he will rumble around in your entrails, but after a while you will see that it was right [to bottle him up.] You will slowly become quiet and change. Then you will discover that there is a stone growing in the bottle ... Insofar as self-control, or non-indulgence, has become a habit, it is a stone ... When that attitude becomes a *fait accompli*, the stone will be a diamond." And the diamond is another image of the *conunctio* [the creation of consciousness]. E. Edinger, *The Mystery of the Conunctio* (Toronto: Inner City Books, 1994), pp. 22—3.

24. A young man with Mars conjunct Pluto informed me that his goal in studying astrology and metaphysics was to gain power over others. He cast spells and actively tried to hurt people. I warned him that his attitude was quite dangerous, that his malevolent intention toward others would be mirrored back to him by the laws of karma and vibrational resonance. The desire to gain control or power over others is not the highest expression of Mars-Pluto. This is one place where the powers of the ego begin to go astray.

25. Mary Plumb, "The Galactic Tree Woman." In *The Mountain Astrologer,* Aug/Sept 2000.

26. Shelley Jordan, personal communication.

27. T. McKenna, *The Archaic Revival: Speculations on Psychedelic Mushrooms, The Amazon, Virtual Reality, UFOs, Shamanism, and the Rebirth of the Goddess* (San Francisco: Harper Collins, 1992).

28. See Chapter 3 for further discussion of Terrence McKenna's chart.

29. Much of this ended up in Andrés' book, *The Wisdom of Sidereal Astrology* (Albuquerque, NM: Sun Publishing, 1983).

30. C. Fagan, *Astrological Origins* (St. Paul, MN: Llewellyn, 1971).

31. See G. Bogart, *The Nine Stages of Spiritual Apprenticeship: Understanding the Student-Teacher Relationship* (Berkeley, CA: Dawn Mountain Press, 1997). Available from Dawn Mountain Press, P.O. Box 9563, Berkeley, CA, USA, 94709; telephone: 510-412-0486.

32. In *The Nine Stages of Spiritual Apprenticeship* I described many of my experiences with Swami Muktananda and his dynamic impact on my life.

33.   Shirdi Sai Baba was born on September 27, 1838 in Pathri Village, India. Source: S. P. Ruhela, *Sri Shirdi Sai Baba: The Universal Master* (New Delhi: Sterling, 1994), p. 1.

34.   S. P. Ruhela, *Sri Shirdi Sai Baba: The Universal Master* (New Delhi: Sterling, 1994), pp. 101—13,   124. Here is how one close disciple described Sai Baba:

"Inwardly, he was as tranquil as the sea ... His state of Self-absorption was constant ... By nature unconceited and very humble, he strove to please all. The words 'Allah Malik' were constantly on his lips. He disliked arguments and unprofitable wranglings ... Somebody's deeds, good or bad, or his innermost secrets were all known to him and he used to astonish devotees by giving a sign or an indication of them ... He was calm and self-restrained, detached and patient, forever in deep meditation; one with the Self and totally absorbed in It; pleased and gracious to his devotees ... Without the least desire for wealth or fame, and alms collection as the sole means of subsistence, he passed his days in this yogic state of withdrawal of all the senses. Whoever went to have his *darshan* would be told the whole secret of his past, future, and present, without his asking for it ... He expected nothing from anyone, but treated them all alike and showered blessings even on those who were ungrateful. Fortune or misfortune, did not disturb his equilibrium." C.Dabholkar, *Shri Sai Satcharita: The Life and Teachings of Shirdi Sai Baba* (New Delhi, Sterling Publishers, 1999), pp. 59, 107, 150–1, 154–5.

35.   H. I. Khan, *The Complete Sayings of Hazrat Inayat Khan* (New Lebanon, NY: Sufi Order Publications, 1991).

36.   For another example illustrating the value of tracking the Saturn cycle, see the example of Nancy in Chapter 4.

37.   D. Rudhyar, *Rhythm of Wholeness* (Wheaton, IL: Quest Books, 1983).

38.   M. L. Von Franz, "The process of individuation". In C. C. Jung, M. L. Von Franz, J. Henderson, J. Jacobi, & A. Jaffe, *Man and His Symbols* (New York: Dell Publishing, 1964), pp. 170–1.

39.   Ibid.

40.   See "Saturn and Uranus: Social Adaptation and Personal Freedom." In G. Bogart, *Therapeutic Astrology* (Berkeley, CA: Dawn Mountain Press, 1996), pp. 165–81.

41.   D. Rudhyar, *Culture, Crisis, and Creativity* (Wheaton, IL: Quest Books, 1977), p. 100.

42. See G. Bogart, *Culture, Crisis, and Creativity: The Prophetic Vision of Dane Rudhyar* (Berkeley, CA: Dawn Mountain Press, 1993).

43. E. Edinger, *The Anatomy of the Psyche* (La Salle, IL: Open Court, 1985), pp. 47ff.

44. H. Hunt, *The Multiplicity of Dreams* (New Haven, CT: Yale University Press, 1989).

45. Ibid.

46. D. Rudhyar, *Rhythm of Wholeness* (Wheaton, IL: Quest Books, 1983), pp. 159–60.

47. See the detailed astrological biography of Mircea Eliade in *Astrology and Spiritual Awakening*.

48. See R. Metzner (Ed.), *Ayahuasca: Hallucinogens, Consciousness, and the Spirit of Nature* (New York: Thunder's Mouth Press, 1999).

49. D. Rudhyar, *Beyond Personhood* (Palo Alto, CA: Rudhyar Institute for Transpersonal Activity, 1982), p. 4.

50. E. Edinger, *Ego and Archetype (Boston:* Shambhala, 1992).

51. Ibid, pp. 69–70.

52. M. L. Von Franz, "The process of Individuation." In C. C. Jung, M. L. Von Franz, J. Henderson, J. Jacobi, & A. Jaffe, *Man and His Symbols* (New York: Dell Publishing, 1964), pp. 164–7.

53. Edward Edinger wrote, "It is definitely not good psychologically always to be a winner, because then one is deprived of the full experience of the opposites. It keeps one superficial. Defeat is the gateway to the unconscious." *The Mystery of the Conunctio* (Toronto: Inner City Books, 1994), p. 16.

54. Sri Aurobindo, *The Synthesis of Yoga* (Pondicherry, India: Sri Aurobindo Ashram, 1965), pp. 51—7. The final paragraph cited is from Sri Aurobindo, *Letters on Yoga* (Pondicherry, India: Sri Aurobindo Ashram, 1971), p. 416. The bracketed additions to the text are mine.

55. D. Rudhyar, *The Astrology of Transformation* (Wheaton, IL: Quest Books, 1980), pp. 151–2.

56. *The Complete Sayings of Hazrat Inayat Khan* (New Lebanon, NY: Sufi Order Publications, 1991).

57. For more on this topic, see "Conscious Suffering," in Chapter 4.

58. See G. Bogart, *Astrology and Spiritual Awakening* (Berkeley, CA: Dawn Mountain Press), pp. 103–5.

59. Sri Aurobindo, *Letters on* Yoga (Pondicherry, India: Sri Aurobindo Ashram, 1971), p. 416.

Chapter 3

60. These were oracular methods used in ancient Greece and Rome.
61. E. Whitmont & S. Perera, *Dreams: A Portal to the Source* (New York: Routledge, 1989).
62. T. Gyatso (The Dalai Lama), *Cultivating a Daily Meditation* (Dharamsala, India: Library of Tibetan Works and Archives, 1991).
63. Ibid, p. 42.
64. Ibid, p. 43.

Chapter 4

65. According to Doctors Edward Hallowell and John Ratey, known side effects of Ritalin include suppression of appetite, loss of sleep, elevated blood pressure or heart rate, nausea, headaches, jitteriness, and, less commonly, involuntary muscle twitches, growth suppression, blocked vision, and impaired memory or motor skills. P. Hallowell & J. Ratey, *Driven to Distraction: Recognizing and Coping with Attention Deficit Disorder* (New York: Touchstone Books, 1994).
66. R. Ebertin, *The Combination of Stellar Influences* (Aalen, Germany: Ebertin Verlag, 1972), p. 163.
67. Sri Aurobindo, "The Hour of God," cited in R. McDermott (Ed.), *The Essential Aurobindo* (New York: Schocken), p.186.
68. E. Edinger, *The Mystery of the Coniunctio* (Toronto: Inner City Books, 1994).

Appendices

69. See E. Edinger, *The Anatomy of the Psyche* (La Salle, IL: Open Court, 1985).
70. M. Baigent, N. Campion, & C. Harvey, *Mundane Astrology: The Astrology of Nations and Groups* (Wellingborough, UK: The Aquarian Press, 1984), p. 184.
71. A. Ruperti, *Cycles of Becoming* (Sebastopol, CA: CRCS Publications, 1978).

72. A. Takra, *The Wisdom of Sidereal Astrology* (Albuquerque, NM: Sun Books, 1983).

73. D. Rudhyar, *Rhythm of Wholeness* (Wheaton, IL: Quest Books, 1983).

Also by The Wessex Astrologer - www.wessexastrologer.com

Patterns of the Past
Karmic Connections
Good Vibrations
The Soulmate Myth: A Dream Come True or Your Worst Nightmare?
The Book of Why
Judy Hall

The Essentials of Vedic Astrology
Lunar Nodes - Crisis and Redemption
Personal Panchanga and the Five Sources of Light
Komilla Sutton

Astrolocality Astrology
From Here to There
Martin Davis

The Consultation Chart
Introduction to Medical Astrology
Wanda Sellar

The Betz Placidus Table of Houses
Martha Betz

Astrology and Meditation
Greg Bogart

The Book of World Horoscopes
Nicholas Campion

Life After Grief : An Astrological Guide to Dealing with Loss
AstroGraphology: The Hidden Link between your Horoscope and your Handwriting
Darrelyn Gunzburg

The Houses: Temples of the Sky
Deborah Houlding

Through the Looking Glass
The Magic Thread
Richard Idemon

Temperament: Astrology's Forgotten Key
Dorian Geiseler Greenbaum

Nativity of the Late King Charles
John Gadbury

Declination - The Steps of the Sun
Luna - The Book of the Moon
Paul F. Newman

Tapestry of Planetary Phases:
Weaving the Threads of Purpose and Meaning in Your Life
Christina Rose

Astrology, A Place in Chaos
Star and Planet Combinations
Bernadette Brady

Astrology and the Causes of War
Jamie Macphail

Flirting with the Zodiac
Kim Farnell

The Gods of Change
Howard Sasportas

Astrological Roots:The Hellenistic Legacy
Between Fortune and Providence: Astrology and the Universe in Dante's
Divine Comedy
Joseph Crane

The Art of Forecasting using Solar Returns
Anthony Louis

Horary Astrology Re-Examined
Barbara Dunn

Living Lilith
M. Kelley Hunter

The Spirit of Numbers: A New Exploration of Harmonic Astrology
David Hamblin

Primary Directions
Martin Gansten

Classical Medical Astrology
Oscar Hofman

The Door Unlocked: An Astrological Insight into Initiation
Dolores Ashcroft Nowicki and Stephanie V. Norris

Understanding Karmic Complexes
Patricia L. Walsh

Pluto Volumes 1 & 2
Jeff Green

Essays on Evolutionary Astrology
Evolutionary Astrology
Jeff Green Edited by Deva Green

Planetary Strength
Bob Makransky

All the Sun Goes Round
Reina James

The Moment of Astrology
Geoffrey Cornelius

The Sacred Dance of Venus and Mars
Michele Finey

CPSIA information can be obtained
at www.ICGtesting.com
Printed in the USA
BVHW040752171019
561335BV00003B/26/P

9 781902 405124